Affordable Heirlooms

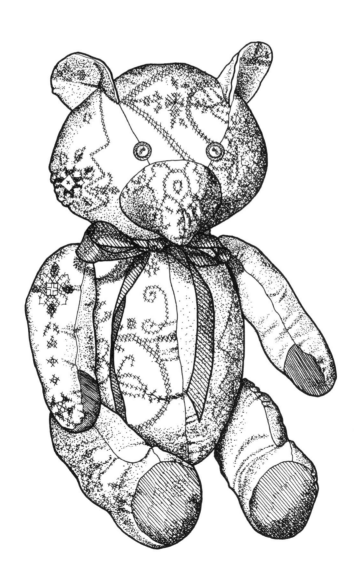

OTHER BOOKS AVAILABLE FROM CHILTON

Robbie Fanning, Series Editor

Contemporary Quilting Series

All Quilt Blocks Are Not Square, by Debra Wagner
Appliqué the Ann Boyce Way, by Ann Boyce
Barbara Johannah's Crystal Piecing, by Barbara Johannah
Complete Book of Machine Quilting, Second Edition,
　　by Robbie and Tony Fanning
Contemporary Quilting Techniques, by Pat Cairns
Creative Triangles for Quilters, by Janet Elwin
Fast Patch, by Anita Hallock
Fourteen Easy Baby Quilts, by Margaret Dittman
Machine-Quilted Jackets, Vests, and Coats, by Nancy Moore
Pictorial Quilts, by Carolyn Hall
Precision-Pieced Quilts Using the Foundation Method,
　　by Jane Hall and Dixie Haywood
Quick-Quilted Home Decor with Your Bernina, by Jackie Dodson
Quick Quilted Home Decor With Your Sewing Machine,
　　by Jackie Dodson
The Quilter's Guide to Rotary Cutting, by Donna Poster
Quilts by the Slice, by Beckie Olson
Scrap Quilts Using Fast Patch, by Anita Hallock
Speed-Cut Quilts, by Donna Poster
Stars Galore and Even More, by Donna Poster
Stitch 'n' Quilt, by Kathleen Eaton
Super Simple Quilts, by Kathleen Eaton
Teach Yourself Machine Piecing and Quilting, by Debra Wagner
Three-Dimensional Appliqué, by Jodie Davis
Three-Dimensional Pieced Quilts, by Jodie Davis

Creative Machine Arts Series

ABCs of Serging, by Tammy Young and Lori Bottom
Alphabet Stitchery by Hand & Machine, by Carolyn Vosburg Hall
The Button Lover's Book, by Marilyn Green
Claire Shaeffer's Fabric Sewing Guide, by Claire Shaeffer
The Complete Book of Machine Embroidery,
　　by Robbie and Tony Fanning
Craft an Elegant Wedding, by Naomi Baker and Tammy Young
Creative Nurseries Illustrated, by Debra Terry and Juli Plooster
Creative Serging Illustrated, The New, by Pati Palmer,
　　Gail Brown, and Sue Green
Distinctive Serger Gifts and Crafts, by Naomi Baker
　　and Tammy Young
The Fabric Lover's Scrapbook, by Margaret Dittman
Friendship Quilts by Hand and Machine, by Carolyn Vosburg Hall
Gail Brown's All-New Instant Interiors, by Gail Brown
Gifts Galore, by Jane Warnick and Jackie Dodson
Hold It! How to Sew Bags, Totes, Duffels, Pouches, and More!,
　　by Nancy Restuccia
How to Make Soft Jewelry, by Jackie Dodson
Innovative Serging, by Gail Brown and Tammy Young
Innovative Sewing, by Gail Brown and Tammy Young
*Owner's Guide to Sewing Machines, Sergers, and Knitting
　　Machines*, by Gale Grigg Hazen
Petite Pizzazz, by Barb Griffin
Putting on the Glitz, by Sandra L. Hatch and Ann Boyce
Quick Napkin Creations, by Gail Brown
Second Stitches, by Susan D. Parker
Serge a Simple Project, by Tammy Young and Naomi Baker
Serge Something Super for Your Kids, by Cindy Cummins

Serged Garments in Minutes, by Tammy Young and Naomi Baker
Sew and Serge Pillows! Pillows! Pillows!, by Jackie Dodson
　　and Jan Saunders
Sew and Serge Terrific Textures, by Jackie Dodson
　　and Jan Saunders
Sew Any Patch Pocket, by Claire Shaeffer
Sew Any Set-In Pocket, by Claire Shaeffer
Sew Sensational Gifts, by Naomi Baker and Tammy Young
Sew, Serge, Press, by Jan Saunders
Simply Serge Any Fabric, by Naomi Baker and Tammy Young
Singer Instructions for Art Embroidery and Lace Work
Soft Gardens, by Yvonne Perez-Collins
The Stretch & Sew Guide to Sewing on Knits, by Ann Person
Twenty Easy Machine-Made Rugs, by Jackie Dodson

Crafts Kaleidoscope

The Banner Book, by Ruth Ann Lowery
Crafter's Guide to Glues, by Tammy Young
Creating and Crafting Dolls, by Eloise Piper and Mary Dilligan
Daddy's Ties, by Shirley Botsford
Dazzle, by Linda Fry Kenzle
Fabric Painting Made Easy, by Nancy Ward
How to Make Cloth Books for Children, by Anne Pellowski
Jane Asher's Costume Book, by Jane Asher
Learn Bearmaking, by Judi Maddigan
Quick and Easy Ways With Ribbon, by Ceci Johnson
Stamping Made Easy, by Nancy Ward
Too Hot to Handle?/Potholders and How to Make Them,
　　by Doris Hoover

StarWear

Embellishments, by Linda Fry Kenzle
Jan Saunders' Wardrobe Quick-Fixes, by Jan Saunders
Make It Your Own, by Lori Bottom and Ronda Chaney
Mary Mulari's Garments With Style, by Mary Mulari
New Serge in Wearable Art, by Ann Boyce
Pattern-Free Fashions, by Mary Lee Trees Cole
Shirley Adams' Belt Bazaar, by Shirley Adams
Sweatshirts With Style, by Mary Mulari

Know Your Sewing Machine Series, by Jackie Dodson

Know Your Bernina, second edition
Know Your Brother, with Jane Warnick
Know Your Elna, with Carol Ahles
Know Your New Home, with Judi Cull and Vicki Lynn Hastings
Know Your Pfaff, with Audrey Griese
Know Your Sewing Machine
Know Your Singer
Know Your White, with Jan Saunders

Know Your Serger Series, by Tammy Young and Naomi Baker

Know Your baby lock
Know Your Serger
Know Your White Superlock

Teach Yourself to Sew Better Series, by Jan Saunders

A Step-by-Step Guide to Your Bernina
A Step-by-Step Guide to Your New Home
A Step-by-Step Guide to Your Sewing Machine
A Step-by-Step Guide to Your Viking

Affordable Heirlooms

*Edna Powers
and Gaye Kriegel*

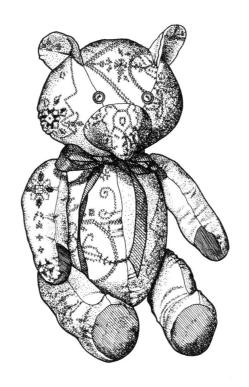

*Chilton Book Company
Radnor, Pennsylvania*

Copyright © 1995
by Edna Powers and Gaye Kriegel

Published in Radnor, Pennsylvania 19089,
by Chilton Book Company

Book design by Heather McLaren

Cover design by Anthony Jacobson

Color photographs by Lee Phillips

Black-and-white photograph
   by Robbie Fanning

Illustrations by Brooke Nolan

Production by Rosalie Cooke

Manufactured in
the United States of America

Library of Congress Cataloging
in Publication Data

Powers, Edna.

   Affordable Heirlooms / Edna Powers
   and Gaye Kriegel.

       p. cm. — (Creative machine arts series)

   Includes bibliographical references and
   index.

   ISBN 0-8019-8647-8 (pbk.)

   1. Dressmaking. 2. Dress accessories.
   3. Textile fabrics in interior decoration.
   4. Household linens—Recycling.
   I. Kriegel, Gaye. II. Title. III. Series.

TT560.P68 1995
746—dc20   95-10550
                                       CIP

1 2 3 4 5 6 7 8 9 0   3 2 1 9 8 7 6 5

The following are registered trademark
names used in this book:

Aleene's	Lastin
Biz	Mountain Mist
Dritz	Orvus
E6000	Pellon
Efferdent	Res-Q Tape
Fairfield	Rit
Fray Check	Seams Great
Gingher	Shaklee
Handler	Stitch Witchery
HeatnBond	Styrofoam
Identipen	Unique Stitch
Ivory Snow	Woolite
Kittrich	

Dedication

From Edna

Mabel Galland Shirk—if ever there were an aunt capable of inspiring this book, it was my Aunt Mabel. Her "make do with what we've got" attitude taught me that the most unusual and wonderful creations are usually found in front of our eyes. Aunt Mabel's love of family and needle arts is truly an heirloom to be passed on to future generations.

From Gaye

To my parents
for a lifetime of encouragement,
to my husband and children
for their patience,
and to my friends for their support.

Contents

"I've been saving crocheted doilies, laces, and unique buttons for years. Much of my stash is from my grandmother's collections. Rather than hiding the treasures, I applied them to a basic linen jacket. I overlapped several doilies in the shoulder and pocket areas and handstitched them in place with buttons added for additional embellishment."
—Nancy Zieman

Foreword

by Robbie Fanning, Series Editor

My husband's mother used to send me rolls of tatted edging. Since I did not know how to tat, the tiny thread loops were like something travelers bring back from foreign countries. *What is it? How do they do it?* I did half-heartedly try to learn how tatting was done, but the woman in the knitting store rolled her eyes and said, "It's very tedious."

I stored the tatted rolls for years in our tiny house, then guiltily gave them away to Goodwill during one of my periodic purges because I didn't know what else to do with them. Now that I've read *Affordable Heirlooms*, I wish I'd either met these authors earlier or had been able to read this book 25 years ago. Not only would I have had help in using the tatting, my tiny house would be even more overflowing because I wouldn't want to purge it of any textile that might transform into clothing, jewelry, toys, curtains, or gifts.

For me, the magic of these Affordable Heirlooms is not so much the end product, but the stories behind the needlework. The work itself evokes questions: who made those tiny French knots? what was she thinking while she worked? was she young? old? single? married? was this her refuge from a hard work day or did she have leisure time during the day?

Another kind of story behind the needlework is the search for the pieces—the wanted ad that produces unwanteds: a trousseau from a busted marriage. Or the friend of a friend whose mother died and when they cleared out the house, your friend rescued tablecloths and linens from the box for Goodwill. Or the drive in the country, stopping at yard sales, looking for textile treasures. The smell of the apple trees, the crunchy crawl down a gravel drive, the tumbling children under the tables, the sense of unexpected adventure—these memories, too, are part of *Affordable Heirlooms.*

Preface

Treasures are hidden in many places—drawers, closets, attics, or basements—and nearly forgotten. Perhaps occasionally you take them out for admiration but then tuck them away again. They can be seen stacked on a shelf at an antique store, bundled in a box at a too-sunny flea market, or tossed on a table at a garage sale. But regardless of their surroundings, the beauty of old linens is undeniable.

Perhaps, like us, you have admired the intricate workmanship lavished on a wide array of old hankies, napkins, tea towels, placemats, and pillowcases. If we have all the timesaving conveniences of contemporary society, why did only they have the time to devote hours to perfecting hand-sewing skills?

For whatever reasons, most of us cannot afford the countless hours required to duplicate these embellishments. However, using basic sewing skills, we can easily manage the minimal time required to incorporate these linens into our sewn garments, accessories, gifts, and home decorating. The results are *Affordable Heirlooms*, and the time-consuming work has been done for us because the embellishment is already on the linen.

You'll notice how most projects in this book take advantage of the linen's finished edges, thereby eliminating the edge treatment necessary when using cut pieces of fabric. If you prefer to skip the construction process altogether, you'll enjoy our ideas on embellishing ready-to-wear. And when you're really pressed for time, many projects actually can be completed in only a few minutes.

Although some of you may shudder at the thought of cutting and re-shaping an old linen for another purpose, we believe that in doing so we honor the women (and girls) who toiled to create these embellishments. Let's rescue these linens from their hiding places, and bring them into the light of day, where they can be used, admired, loved, and passed on to yet another generation.

Some of your inherited linens may indeed be too precious to alter. If so, use them for projects that do not require the linens to be cut. (These are noted with the symbol ✄ throughout the book.) Or purchase either old or new linens and proceed freely without the hindrance of emotional attachment.

There are a few constraints when working with old linens, such as avoiding holes, creases, or stains, but these challenges are inconsequential compared to the rewards. Through *Affordable Heirlooms*, we recycle, reuse, and remember the timeless beauty of handwork from a bygone era.

Introduction

A few suggestions to help you use this book:

- Forget the linen's intended purpose—placemat, napkin, or towel. Instead, evaluate each linen as to how to showcase its embellishment and how to save time by using its prefinished edges.

- Read through all instructions before beginning a project. General sewing techniques are not explained due to space constraints, so consult other resources, if necessary.

- Basic sewing tools such as sewing machine, scissors, and pins are assumed to be available, and are not listed for each project.

- Keep every scrap from projects in progress, to use for collage and jewelry projects, or for experiments with glues, dyes, and decorative stitches.

- Familiarize yourself with all the ways these projects work around damaged linens. Some of the best bargains available are somewhat damaged linens that the owner does not know how to use. You may want to buy a damaged linen that has a still usable lace or edging.

- Start with and maintain clean hands, tools, and work surfaces, to avoid soiling linens.

- Use fine threads and fine *new* needles for fine fabrics.

Helpful definitions:

baste – Sew with a longer than average stitch length. To baste for gathering, stitch with the right side of the fabric up—then pull the bobbin thread to gather.

edgestitch – Stitch on the uppermost fabric layer less than 1/8" from garment edge.

French seam – Sew fabric first with wrong sides together; then trim, refold, and sew with right sides together, encasing first portion of seam allowance.

pivot – With machine needle in fabric, lift presser foot and change fabric's position; then lower presser foot and continue sewing.

tack – Sew simple hand stitches which can easily be removed later, if desired.

topstitch – Stitch on the uppermost fabric layer 1/8" or more from garment edge.

underlining – To provide stability and opaqueness, baste underlining to the underside of the fabric or linen, then handle both layers as one.

understitch – Sew facing to seam allowance underneath to flatten seam and to help prevent facing from rolling out.

Illustration symbols:

RS - right side
WS - wrong side
SA - seam allowance
⊗ - project does not require linen to be cut

Finding and Caring for Linens

Perhaps you've inherited a collection of beautiful linens, all in pristine condition and properly stored over the years, so they're ready to use. If not, you'll find many useful tips in this section for acquiring, preparing, and maintaining linens for your projects.

Finding Linens

Most of us enjoy fabric shopping—we're easily entertained by color, texture, and bargains. Shopping for linens is all that and more because you'll go to unusual places (perhaps at early morning hours you never knew existed), meet interesting people (who often know the history of the linens they're selling), and find unique linens (each one different than the next). Then you can still go shopping for fabric to coordinate with your linens!

Begin your search by asking relatives and friends for linens that they may have no use for (unless they've seen this book). Ask others to watch for linens and alert you.

Old linens may be offered at garage sales, flea markets, auctions, estate sales, and thrift shops. Unfold and examine them carefully, as purchases are final. Go early, go often, and take cash in small denominations. (It's awkward to offer $3 for a linen and then hand over a $20 bill.)

Some antique shops sell or even specialize in linens. (Check back every couple of months, and also ask the owner to notify you when something special arrives.) Read your newspaper classifieds, or place a "wanted" advertisement.

New linens are available at many fabric, craft, and lace shops, bed and bath boutiques, and department stores. Mail order is yet another option. (See Resources, page 115.)

Cleaning Linens

Just as you prewash your fabric, it's nice to have all your linens clean, so they'll be ready when you are. Treat old linens gently, since they are more fragile, and are more likely to be stained than new linens.

Always begin the cleaning process with the mildest method. If you have any doubt about the linen's stability, wash it by hand. Use a gentle touch though, as linens are weaker when wet. Most sources agree that Biz is one of the best and safest products to use for cleaning linens. (Drop by either of our kitchens and you're likely to see the perpetual bucket of Biz with new linen finds soaking inside.) Do not use Biz on silk or wool, however, as it can damage them.

Be sure to rinse linens thoroughly, then soak in plain water to rinse again,—and again, if necessary. Detergent residue can scorch when ironed or can yellow over time, according to Michele Clise, author of *The Linen Closet: How to Care for Your Fine Linens and Lace.* (See Bibliography, page 115.)

Only the sturdiest of cotton linens should you consider machine-washing, and even then, use a gentle cycle, lingerie bag, and mild detergent such as Ivory Snow, Orvus, or Woolite.

Stubborn stains may simply require more soaking time, even days if necessary, changing sudsy water repeatedly. Rust stains from pins are a common problem. Consider the rust remover by Rit (located with the dye packages), or a paste made from cream of tartar and a few drops of water. Other brown stains that look like rust may actually have been caused by direct contact with wood. All woods, even cedar, have the potential to stain fabric.

For additional whitening, consider Rit white-wash, Shaklee Nature-Bright, or Efferdent (although there's a risk of tiny blue stains if Efferdent is not fully dissolved).

Chlorine bleach should be avoided, due to its caustic nature. The damage bleach causes to fibers may not show immediately, but old linens could eventually disintegrate. Also be cautious of using a professional dry cleaner. You may not care for their chemicals, and they certainly won't care for your linens as gently as you would.

Air-drying (either hanging from a line, or laying flat on a towel) is substantially less risky than machine-drying. There's an old wives' tale about whitening linens by drying them in the sunshine on a grass lawn or on a snowbank (depending on where you live). Does it work? Perhaps, but only if the linens are safe from animals and children.

Before going to extremes that may cause more harm than good, decide how clean is clean enough. Old linens don't have to look new—there's nothing wrong with old and proud, and soiled is better than shredded.

But if the color is still not pleasing, consider dying the linen, using a commercial dye or a tea solution. In both cases, wet the linen with plain water first.

Persistent stains or actual holes in linens necessitate creative effort to cut around or cut out; to incorporate into seams, tucks, or folds; or to cover with buttons, bows, lace, or another linen. Since the problems are as individual as the linens, you may have to try several of these ideas or perhaps change to another project before reaching a satisfactory result.

Pressing Linens

When did ironing get such a bad reputation? Pressing can be meditative, especially while listening to music. If you have a real aversion to the iron, choose *Affordable Heirlooms* projects that do not require repeated washing and, therefore, repeated pressing. Whatever amount of pressing you do, console yourself that it's a fraction of the time spent by earlier generations—and we have modern equipment.

Be sure your iron and ironing surfaces are immaculate, or you might stain the linen you just worked so hard to clean. Also clean the inside of the iron, to avoid mineral spots. Steam, water spray, and starch significantly help to control wrinkles.

Take care that the iron's tip does not catch in lace or embroidered openings. Press raised lace and embroidery, right side down, on a folded diaper, Turkish towel, or other soft cloth. (Metallic ironing board covers are too harsh.) The embroidery will sink into the folded cloth, allowing the iron's surface to touch the surrounding fabric.

When linens need to be squared, dampen first, then press on a grid surface, or shape and pin to a cloth-covered foam-core board, and let dry.

Storing Linens

Our first suggestion is to not store them at all—use them instead. But when you must store linens, put them away clean, not ironed, and without starch, because starch attracts bugs. Wrap linens in acid-free *white* tissue paper (see Resources, page 115) or in clean sheets.

Never wrap linens in plastic, as trapped moisture can cause mildew or yellowing.

Never lay linens in direct contact with wood, as sap can stain. Never store linens dirty, as newer stains are easier to clean. Never use *blue* acid-free tissue paper, as the color can transfer to linens, according to Kaethe Kliot, owner of Lacis. (See Resources, page 115.)

Refold linens periodically to limit constant stress on the same creases. Avoid temperature extremes or direct sunlight.

"**D**on't harness your thoughts to a linen's original purpose. Explore the possibilities of each linen based on its size, shape, color, embellishment, and condition."
—*Gaye Kriegel*

"**O**ne morning two friends and I leafed through a newly purchased box of old linens. Trash or treasure? One friend was as excited as I was about the possibilities—but the other said, 'Yuk!' and raced away to wash her hands."
—*Edna Powers*

No-Sew Ideas ✂

Until there's opportunity in your busy schedule to begin your first of many *Affordable Heirlooms* projects, try any of the following suggestions that do not require you to measure, cut, or sew.

Drape linens over:

- tables, alone or over another table skirt
- shelves
- mantles
- curtains
- lamps
- chair or sofa backs
- stools or piano benches
- colorful terrycloth towels
- an old-fashioned clothes rack

Put linens in:

- baskets
- trays
- bowls
- jacket or jeans pockets
- flower vases, partially draped over the top edge

Place linens under:

- lamp bases
- centerpieces
- candlesticks
- jacket lapels
- a jacket, as a faux camisole

Tie linens around:

- dried or silk flowers
- teapot or pitcher handles
- scented cotton balls or non-oil potpourri

Pin linens on:

- tops of pincushions
- garments or pillows, using a jewelry pin

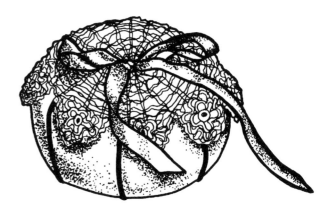

Part I
Clothing

Throughout the ages, people have adorned their bodies with whatever they considered beautiful—fur skins, draped linen, lace ruff collars, enormous hoopskirts, or miniskirts. Although ideals of fashion beauty are forever evolving, most forms of needlework, such as lace, drawnwork, and cutwork, seem to elude time and remain classically beautiful. The use and extent of embellishment may change, but the inherent beauty of fine threads, exquisite workmanship, and subtle colors withstands the test of time.

The tradition of adornment continues as we find pleasure including these past treasures into our present wardrobe—and ponder who will wear them again in succeeding generations.

Many of our clothing projects use purchased patterns, but the Nightgown (page 14) can be made without a pattern. Lots of ideas are presented which substitute linens for only part of a garment and use linens to embellish readymade clothes. The general information in our *Using Linens for Apparel* section will help guide all your *Affordable Heirlooms* clothing projects.

Using Linens for Apparel

The style of the linen and its embellishment determine the garment's character, just as selecting a particular fabric would. There's such a wide variety of linens available, you'll find something to suit any garment, from casual to dressy; and to complement any fabric, from denim to velvet.

Since the size of the linen is predetermined, you must be willing to try some unusual cutting layouts and creative piecing, and you must definitely be willing to iron. This extra planning pays off later, as the linen's finished edges eliminate some construction steps, such as hems, seam finishes, and closure plackets.

Preshrink all washable linens and fabrics. Linens will probably need to be starched, and may need to be squared during pressing. Linens and fabrics that are permanently attached to each other must have compatible care needs. If one or the other cannot be washed, consider detachable techniques.

Since linens are often white and somewhat transparent, some construction techniques in the pattern's guide sheet may need to be changed. For example, if a facing shows through a linen, consider lining, bias facing, or bias binding instead. Also, use caution before placing a single layer transparent linen over another fabric, as the look may not be pleasing.

Embellishment added to a garment does not have to be symmetrical, but should be balanced. After pinning embellishments onto the garment, hang it where you can stand back and evaluate the effect. If possible, try on the garment to see if it's flattering, and try not to make a snap decision. Adding similar topstitching, trims, or buttons to other parts of the garment or to accessories may help to achieve a cohesive look.

Since many linens are not replaceable —and cutting is so permanent—if you have any doubts about size, design, or technique, make a muslin sample. Mark embellishment location on the muslin, then practice with the sample before using the actual linen.

A typical pattern piece covers only half the body. It must be cut either twice or on the fold. When working with unusual cutting layouts, you're less likely to make a mistake if you take a few minutes to make a *complete pattern* for key pieces.

Trace the pattern accurately onto your preferred type of pattern paper, including notches, grainline, and other pertinent notations. (See Resources, page 115, for our favorite pattern paper.) Then cut out, turn over, and tape to the original pattern along center line. Mark seam allowances on pattern, so that as you manipulate the linen, you see exactly what will be included in the finished garment.

"My grandmother, Ida Koski, trimmed a linen handkerchief with orange variegated thread and crocheted a dainty butterfly in one corner. If the butterfly makes a perfect accent on a garment, I'll cut the hankie apart. I don't think my grandmother would gasp or cry. I believe she too would re-use her older handwork in new, up-to-date ways, and would encourage me to do the same."
—Mary Mulari, author, Mary Mulari's Garments With Style

All-Linen Garments

The challenge of making an entire garment from linens is finding large enough pieces. Possible choices include pillowcases, tablecloths, curtains, sheets, and European guest towels. Smaller matching or coordinating linens may supplement for sleeves and collars.

European guest towels are smooth cotton linens, embellished on one end. They're available through mail order (see Resources, page 115), and only in white, but, of course, you could dye them. Before preshrinking, the large towel is approximately 28" x 44" and the small towel is approximately 14" x 22". Use them individually as accents, or combine them for increased usable width and length.

Mother/Daughter Dresses

Sure to delight both mother and daughter, these coordinating dresses are both made from embellished linens, yet styled to be appropriate for the individual.

Please read *Using Linens for Apparel,* page 6.

Supplies: Mother's Dress

- 2 large European guest towels (see above)
- 2 small European guest towels
- commercial sheath-style dress pattern
- additional items, as noted on pattern

Procedure

1 First decide the garment's finished length. The body measurement from shoulder to desired hem point must match the dress front pattern measurement from shoulder (excluding seam allowance) to bottom edge (excluding hem allowance). Lengthen or shorten front and back patterns as necessary, working within linen's parameter.

2 Fold each large towel lengthwise, centering an

embroidery motif; then cut garment front and back, with pattern hem allowances folded away.

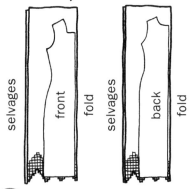

3 Cut shaped facings from leftover linen pieces.

Or substitute facings with an alternate technique, such as bias binding, bias facings, or lining.

4 Lay the two small towels with right sides together and embellished ends together. Fold up sleeve pattern hem allowance, disregarding any curve along pattern's lower edge. Pin pattern to towels, aligning sleeve's lower folded edge with towels' embellished edges; then cut sleeves. (If small towels are

not wide enough for sleeves, either substitute two large towels or cut plain sleeves from one large towel.)

5 Continue garment construction, omitting references to dress and sleeve hems.

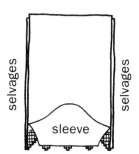

Supplies:
Daughter's Dress

- 3 large European guest towels (see page 7)
- commercial pattern with fitted bodice and full skirt

- additional fabric for bodice lining or facings, optional
- additional items, as noted on pattern

For a smaller daughter, two European guest towels may provide enough skirt fullness. You'll have two side seams, and will need a back placket for closure.

Procedure

1 Determine garment's finished length. The body measurement from waist to desired hem point must match the skirt front pattern measurement from waist (excluding seam allowance) to bottom edge (excluding hem allowance). Lengthen or shorten pattern as necessary.

2 Stack the towels with their embellished ends together. Lay skirt front pattern (hem allowance folded away) on stacked towels, aligning the folded pattern edge with embellished ends. Before cutting across pattern top, plan ahead so that sufficient fabric remains for other pattern pieces.

3 Fold one leftover towel piece in half with selvages together, to cut bodice front and sleeve binding. Cut bodice back and sleeves from remaining two leftover towel pieces. (You will need additional fabric for optional bodice lining or facings.)

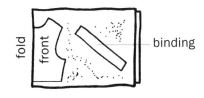

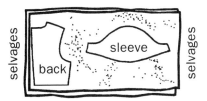

4 During assembly, note that by using three pieces for skirt, one seam will be positioned at center back, and the other seams at side front. The midpoint between the side-front seams is the center front. (See Night-gown diagram, pages 14 and 15.) When joining skirt pieces, leave open the placket portion of center back seam. Towel selvages eliminate further seam finishes; and by pressing both center back seam allowances to the left, sewn placket is eliminated.

5 Continue garment construction, omitting reference to dress hem. If you look ahead in the book, you'll find many choices for collars that could be added to this dress. Or keep the dress neckline plain and accessorize with our detachable collars or with the Heart's Desire Pendant on page 41.

"**F**or my seventh birthday my grandmother gave me a sewing basket brimming with supplies including two pillowcases that were printed with designs to embroider, embroidery floss, a hoop, thimble (which I still use today), scissors, and needles. Then she taught me the basics of hand embroidery. I didn't consider those pillowcases to be heirlooms when I was seven, but I truly wish I had them now. I would encourage everyone to save their first projects as a comforting reminder of where we first began."
— Jan Saunders, co-author, Sew & Serge Series

Pillowcase Dress

What sweeter way to clothe a baby or toddler than in a linen that has been so well cared for through the years that it has developed a buttery smoothness? A new pillowcase may be used instead, but be sure that you wash and dry it several times, to avoid irritating a child's tender skin.

By using a pillowcase for the skirt portion of the dress, the side seams, hem, and embellishment are already done for you. Although the entire dress can be made from a single pillowcase, a matching pillowcase provides more fabric and embellishment options for bodice, sleeves, or collar.

Entirely different looks can be achieved, depending on the pillowcase embellishment and the finished garment length—from short/casual to long/christening.

Please read *Using Linens for Apparel,* page 6.

Supplies

- 1 embellished pillowcase
- commercial pattern with high bodices front and back
- additional items, as noted on pattern

Procedure

1 On front/back skirt pattern piece, fold away side seam and any angle that side seam may have, so there is a right angle at the underarm.

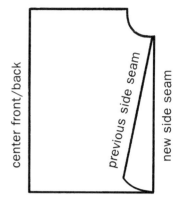

2 Also fold away pattern's hem allowance.

3 If there is only a half-pattern for the skirt (a center front/back edge and one side seam), it's helpful to make a complete pattern (see page 6), but keep these two pieces separate.

4 There's little chance that dress pattern width will exactly match pillowcase width. Although you could narrow the pillowcase by sewing side seams, you'd risk distracting from or actually ruining the embellishment. A better solution is to alter the pattern to correspond to the width of the pillowcase. (See next page.) The only effect of this alteration is that more gathers would be fitted to the bodice.

Position each pattern's folded side edge at pillowcase side edges. Regardless of whether pattern pieces meet each other at center front, you will later cut straight across the top edge. The center front/back corresponds to midpoint of pillowcase.

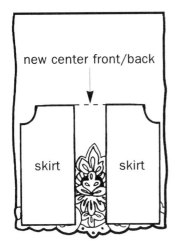

new center front/back

skirt skirt

If pattern is wider than pillowcase, some ease could be sacrificed by folding out excess pattern.

5 The garment's finished length must be decided at this time. You may place each pattern's folded hemline on pillowcase's embellished bottom edge, or alter garment length by moving pattern piece up or down pillowcase.

skirt skirt

6 Before cutting, lay out additional pattern pieces (bodice, sleeves, etc.) on remaining portion of pillowcase, to be sure there is sufficient space.

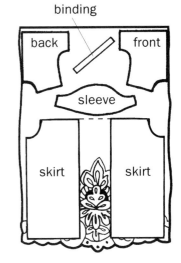

binding

back front

sleeve

skirt skirt

7 Continue garment construction, omitting references to side seams and hem. If embroidery is too open, attach a lining at bodice/skirt seam, or have child wear a slip.

*"**W**hen my grandmother hit 90 years of age, she decided that each of the women in the family needed a dozen pillowcases with crocheted edges (the only kind you should ever sleep on) and a dozen pair of hand-knit mittens for our families—in case she died suddenly and we didn't have time to do these things for ourselves. This incredible endeavor didn't faze her in the least. That was over 30 years ago and I still have one mitten left. I only have to look at it to get a warm feeling."*

—Jackie Dodson, co-author, Sew & Serge Series

Pillowcase Petticoat

A pair of matching pillowcases makes a pretty petticoat. To wear the petticoat under more than one garment, sew an elastic casing at the waistline. Or follow these directions to attach a petticoat permanently under a dress. You could choose to make a petticoat with the pillowcase embellishment worn at the front and back, but for our sample garment the pillowcase embellishment was positioned at the sides. The pleating at each side of the dress allows more of the petticoat's embellishment to show. Please read *Using Linens for Apparel,* page 6.

Supplies

- 2 matching pillowcases
- optional ribbon
- commercial dress pattern
- dress fabric
- additional items, as noted on pattern

Procedure

1 After cutting dress fabric, use skirt front pattern for petticoat, but fold away all but 1/2" of the hem allowance. The petticoat will then be 1/2" longer than dress. Lay pattern on each pillowcase, and cut off excess at pillowcase upper seamed edge.

2 Refold each pillowcase so embellishment is positioned at side. Cut each pillowcase open along the fold opposite embellishment.

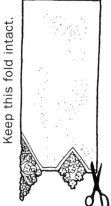

Keep this fold intact.

3 Measure total finished width of skirt by adding together front and back skirt pattern widths, less seam allowances. Seam the two pillowcases, right sides together, adjusting seam allowance amount to make finished width of skirt and petticoat equal. If dress is not a pullover style, use skirt back pattern to mark center back closure position; then leave petticoat seam open above that mark.

4 Since petticoat seams are located at center front and back, you may want to cover the seams with an edgestitched ribbon. Match ribbon color to pillowcase color, to be less conspicuous.

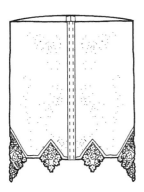

5 After skirt is sewn, position petticoat to skirt, both right sides up, aligning petticoat seams to skirt's center front and back. Join layers at upper edges, as you sew gathering threads.

6 Continue garment construction. When skirt is hemmed, it will be 1/2" shorter than petticoat. To show even more pillowcase embellishment, finger-pleat the dress several inches shorter at each side seam. Hand-sew pleats together, and accent with ribbon or fabric bow.

"These 50-year-old pillowcases were crocheted for me by my patient when I worked for 50 cents an hour as a private-duty nurse. Because my mother was a professional seamstress, my nursing uniform was my very first ready-made garment."
—Elizabeth Bringmann, age 85

Nightgown

Sweet dreams will enfold you while slumbering in this lovely nightgown of pleasing comfort and old-world charm. The sewing is so simple, you won't need a pattern. Please read *Using Linens for Apparel,* page 6.

Supplies

- 3 large European guest towels, see page 7
- 1 small European guest towel
- 3/4 yard single-fold bias tape

Using size of towel specified, finished width at lower edge is 81"; finished length from top of bodice (not top of strap) is 46". (Directions follow to shorten gown.) A narrower gown could be made from two large towels.

Finished width of front bodice is: size 6–8, 10-1/2"; size 10–12, 11-1/2"; size 14–16, 12-1/2"; size 18–20, 13-1/2".

Procedure

1 Prewash, dry, and press linens. Cut off hemmed edge of each large towel.

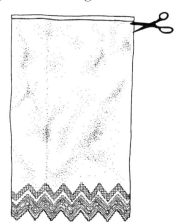

2 For skirt portion of nightgown, align embellished edges of the large towels, and seam together lengthwise, right sides together, with a 1/2"-wide seam allowance. Towel selvages provide seam finish.

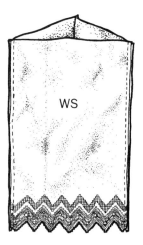

WS

3 Select one seam as the center back. The other two seams will be side-front seams. The midpoint between the side-front seams is the center front. Lay skirt flat, matching center front and back. Smooth skirt out to each side and press creases at skirt top to denote sides.

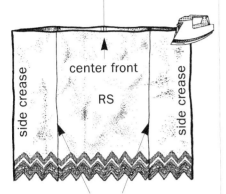

center back seam

center front

RS

side crease

side crease

side front seams

4 Since the towel's embellished edge will serve as the hemline, the nightgown's finished length must be decided now. If desired, trim straight across upper edge to shorten length.

5 Trace and trim (on appropriate size line) the underarm template from page 17. Pin template to skirt upper edge at side crease, and cut along curved line of template. Turn template over to repeat cutting step for other underarm.

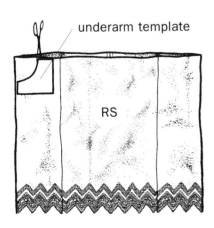

underarm template

RS

6 To finish underarm curve, open one folded edge of bias tape and pin to garment, right sides together, cut edges even. Ease tape around curve by *slightly* stretching tape and letting the tape's seam allowance ripple. Stitch along tape crease line.

RS underarm

7 Clip seam allowances every 3/8", turn tape to underside, press flat, and edgestitch close to tape's remaining free edge.

WS underarm

8 Sew two rows of basting across upper edges of skirt front and back. The first row should be 3/8" from cut edge, and the second row 5/8" from cut edge.

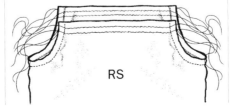

RS

9 Cut a 4"-wide strip off each end of small towel. The embellished end will become the bodice front band and the hemmed end (including the hem itself) will be used for the bodice back band. Cut two more 4"-wide strips across small towel, and set aside for straps.

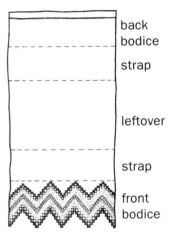

back bodice

strap

leftover

strap

front bodice

10 Select a center motif, scallop, etc., from embellished strip. Trim ends of bodice front and back strips to the following lengths: size 6–8, 11-1/2"; size 10–12, 12-1/2"; size 14–16, 13-1/2"; size 18–20, 14-1/2".

11 Pin cut edge of bodice front to skirt front, right sides together, matching centers, and having bodice extend 1/2" past skirt at each side. Pull up bobbin threads and distribute gathers evenly. Sew across gathers in a 1/2"-wide seam allowance. To finish seam allowance, either serge or zigzag close to seam-line, and then trim close to zigzag. Press seam allowance toward bodice, and topstitch.

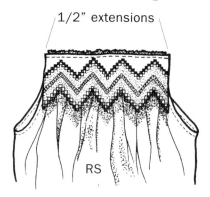
1/2" extensions

RS

12 Repeat construction steps, to join bodice back and skirt back.

13 Press under the 1/2"-wide extensions on each side of bodice front and back, to become even with bias-finished underarms.

14 The short ends of straps are selvages that do not require finishing. Sew long sides of each strap, right sides together, with a 1/4"-wide seam allowance. Press seam allowance open.

WS

15 Turn each strap right side out. Rotate the strap, so the seam allowance is under the middle of the strap, and press flat. Zigzag or serge short ends closed.

RS

zigzag   seam allowance

16 Pin right side of each strap against wrong side of bodice front, covering bodice's pressed-under side edges. The strap ends will be even with bodice front/skirt seam.

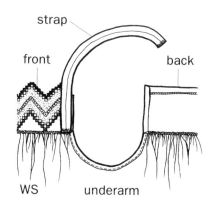
strap

front   back

WS   underarm

17 Secure straps to bodice front by topstitching a rectangle on bodice through all thicknesses. Vary stitching line to follow shape of embellishment, if appropriate.

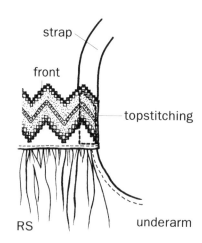
strap

front

topstitching

RS   underarm

18 Try on nightgown to determine finished strap length. Then repeat placement and topstitching steps to attach back ends of straps

to bodice back. Retain any excess strap extending below back bodice/skirt seam, for possible lengthening later (particularly for a child's nightgown), or zigzag over ends and trim to shorten.

See template next page.

*"**M**y mother's hands were never idle—she was always making something. Her friends visited daily to chat as they did their needlework. In this small New Mexico town during the 1930s, these ladies had to depend on the Sears Roebuck mail-order catalog for materials. When a women's magazine arrived (their only source of ideas and patterns) they excitedly gathered around the one copy to see what was new."*
—Edith Forsling

Nightgown Underarm Template

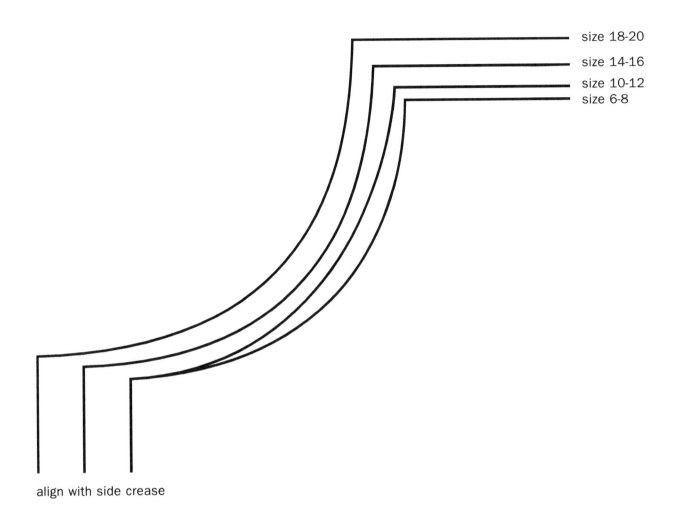

size 18-20

size 14-16

size 10-12
size 6-8

align with side crease

Linen Accents

If an all-linen garment doesn't appeal to you, try adding a linen accent to a garment. Collars, cuffs, yokes, and pocket tops are garment areas easily substituted by, or highlighted with, a linen. Since fabric and linen are attached to each other, their care needs must be identical.

Blouse Overlays and Cuffs

Three embellished hankies take a tailored blouse from traditional to timeless. Hankies need not be identical, but might share a common element, such as the same embroidery color. Select a fabric to match or complement hankies. Shoulder overlays will be positioned straighter on the body if pattern has set-in sleeves, rather than a drop-shoulder style. Please read *Using Linens for Apparel,* page 6.

Supplies

- 3 hankies
- commercial blouse pattern
- blouse fabric
- additional items, as noted on pattern

Procedure

1 Cut blouse from fabric. Remove blouse front pattern, and temporarily pin fabric fronts together along center line. Clean and starch hankies. Pin one hankie over each blouse shoulder, making sure hankie edges are straight, level with each other, and an equal distance from center front. Trim hankies along neck, shoulder, and sleeve edges.

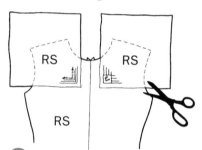

2 Baste cut edges together inside seam allowances. Finished hankie edges may be left as is or topstitched to blouse using a narrow zigzag.

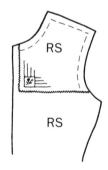

3 If stabilized with an underlining of blouse fabric, hankies (excluding their delicate edges) may be used for cuffs. Cut cuff pattern from blouse fabric, preferably on bias grain. Set fabric cuffs aside.

4 Mark seam allowance lines on cuff pattern (if they're not already there) to better visualize what will be seen on the finished cuff. Cut the third hankie in half, then position halves right sides together with cut edges aligned. Pin pattern onto hankie halves, planning for nicest embroidery to be on cuff overlap (buttonhole end). Trim excess hankie along pattern.

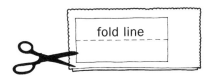

5 Baste together the fold line of each hankie cuff and its fabric underlining. Press fold line so that underlining layers are inside of hankie layers. Trim any excess underlining around hankie perimeter. Unfold cuff, pin or baste outside edges together, and then handle as one layer.

6 Continue blouse construction. Our garment shown on page 18 and photo #3 has a front band and collar topstitched with a decorative stitch and wing needle to complement hankie embroidery. To avoid marring cuff embroidery, bias-cut fabric loops or thread loops may replace sewn buttonholes.

"I once designed a bed cover using recycled floral hankies—lovely I thought. It photographed beautifully for Handmade *magazine. But my husband didn't agree: "Who would ever want to sleep under all those hankies considering the noses they've blown?"*
—Gail Brown, author, Gail Brown's Instant Interiors

Shirt Collar and Pocket Top

A hot roll cover does a better job of embellishing a garment than keeping rolls hot. It's common for this linen style to have three identical corners and one larger, more embellished corner. Use three corners to make a collar, and the fourth corner to decorate a pocket top. Please read *Using Linens for Apparel*, page 6.

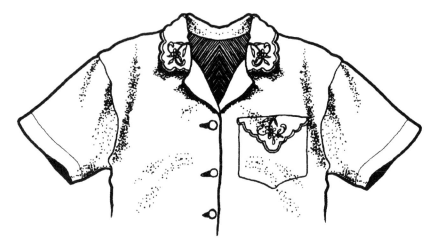

Supplies

- 1 hot roll cover
- commercial shirt pattern with convertible collar
- shirt fabric
- additional items, as noted on pattern

Procedure

1 Clean and starch hot roll cover, then cut a square from each corner.

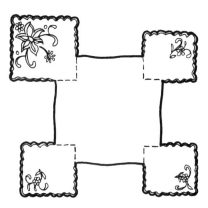

2 If collar pattern is only a half-pattern, make a complete pattern according to page 6.

3 Pin two small linen squares on short ends of collar pattern, positioning each square's finished edges inside seam allowance lines.

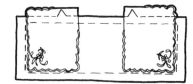

4 Turn large linen square diagonally and pin to collar pattern center, overlapping smaller squares and extending past pattern style line. Trim excess linen squares

only along neck edge, retaining notches. *Do not* cut along collar style line.

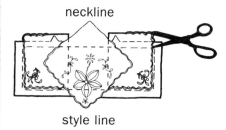

neckline

style line

5 Remove pattern, but keep collar squares pinned together. Join squares by topstitching a narrow zigzag along middle square's finished edges. Carefully trim along zigzag stitches the portion of the smaller squares that extends under large square.

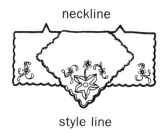

neckline

style line

6 Baste collar to garment neckline, both right sides up, matching center backs and fronts. Collar neckline will be finished simultaneously with shirt neckline.

7 Fold away pocket pattern's hem allowance. Cut shirt fabric using adjusted pocket pattern.

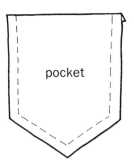

8 Press under seam allowances on fabric pocket. Pin remaining small linen

corner to pocket, both right sides up. Cut off excess linen, 1" above pocket top, then serge or zigzag this cut edge.

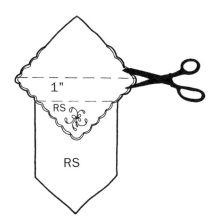

9 Narrowly zigzag linen's finished edge to pocket. Press under linen corners flush with pocket sides, then press the 1" linen extension underneath upper pocket edge. Topstitch pocket to shirt, and continue garment construction.

"This linen hot roll cover was a wedding gift along with a silver tray. I've still never used the tray but the linen made a cute collar for what would have been an ordinary shirt."
—Gaye Kriegel

Placemat Collar and Cuffs

Two hemstitched linen placemats provide enough fabric for collar, cuffs, corded piping, covered buttons, and a matching headband. Please read *Using Linens for Apparel,* page 6.

Supplies

- 2 placemats
- commercial dress pattern with high bodices front and back
- dress fabric
- additional items, as noted on pattern

Procedure

1 Make a complete front bodice pattern. (See page 6.)

2 Clean and starch placemats; then cut one placemat in half, crosswise.

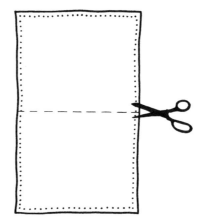

3 To make the collar, pin one of the placemat halves over front bodice pattern.

Adjust collar length either to show or cover bodice/skirt seam. Trim placemat along neck and shoulders.

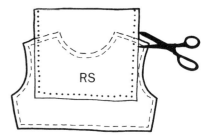

4 Cut the other placemat half in half again, crosswise.

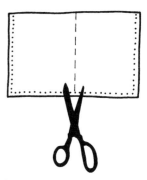

5 Put these two placemat pieces right sides together, and pin them to back bodice pattern, adjusting shoulder width and collar length to match the already cut front collar. Trim placemat pieces along neck, shoulder, and, if necessary, center back edge.

6 French-seam collar front to back at shoulders,

pressing seam allowances toward front. Narrowly hem each collar back edge, using the 5/8" seam allowance. Baste collar to bodice neckline, both right sides up, matching center fronts and shoulder seams. Collar neckline will be finished simultaneously with dress neckline.

7 Fold cuff pattern along fold line, then fold away seam allowances at short ends.

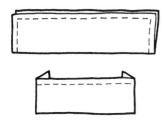

8 Pin cuff pattern's long folded edge to a short end of second placemat. Cut all the way across placemat end. Repeat to cut second cuff across opposite placemat end.

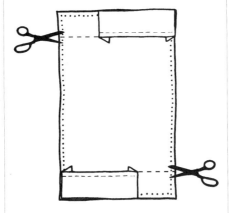

9 If placemat piece is longer than cuff pattern, press the extra amount to wrong side, on cuff underlap (button) end. Tack this folded amount, or fuse, using paper-backed fusible web.

10 Sew each cuff to prepared sleeve edge. Serge, or trim and bind this seam allowance, since it will not be concealed in a cuff facing. To reinforce single fabric layer, pin two rectangles of non-woven interfacing under each cuff buttonhole area. Sew buttonholes; then trim interfacing close to stitching.

11 From remaining center section of placemat, cut optional bias strips for corded piping, bias cover for Padded Headband (see page 50), and scraps to cover buttons for cuffs. Continue garment construction.

"I spent 50 cents for these two peach linen placemats at a garage sale about nine years ago. Two years after that I found a perfect floral print to match them and made my daughter this dress. Little did I know that my interest in using old linens would snowball into writing this book!"

—Gaye Kriegel

V-Neck Collar

A simple "V" neckline is suddenly stunning with the addition of a beautiful lace-edged hankie. You'll see dramatic results with virtually no effort because the linen does it all. Please read *Using Linens for Apparel,* page 6.

Supplies

- 1 lace-edged hankie
- commercial dress pattern with high front bodice and V-neck
- dress fabric
- additional items, as noted on pattern

Procedure

1 Mark seam allowance lines on front bodice pattern. Clean and starch hankie; then cut it in half.

2 Pin hankie halves right sides together, and cut edges even. Lay them over front bodice pattern. If hankie pieces extend past sleeve seam allowance, reduce hankie width by

trimming from previously cut hankie edges.

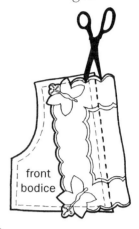

3 If hankie pieces extend into shoulder and lower seam allowances, lengthen bodice front (and back) patterns accordingly.

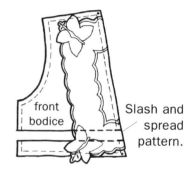

4 After cutting garment, baste one hankie piece to each bodice front, both right sides up. Collar neckline will be finished simultaneously with dress neckline.

5 Continue garment construction. Tack each collar's upper edge invisibly to garment shoulder seams to prevent collars from falling away from dress.

Seamless Collar

Select this technique for a collar when you prefer *not* to cut through the linen's side edges. This collar may be added to many styles of dresses or blouses. If you prefer to keep it separate from the garment, finish its neckline with one of the upcoming detachable techniques. Please read *Using Linens for Apparel,* page 6.

Supplies

- 1 embellished placemat, tea towel, or small European guest towel (see page 7)
- commercial dress or blouse pattern with jewel neckline and one-piece collar
- dress or blouse fabric
- additional items, as noted on pattern

Procedure

1 Clean and starch linen, then fold it in half lengthwise. Determine front collar length by moving pattern up or down linen's fold. Cut neck and center back pattern edges; then cut straight over to linen's hemmed sides. *Do not* cut collar pattern's style line.

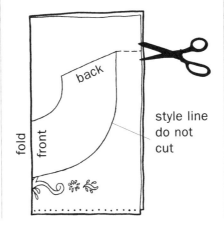

2 Narrowly hem center back and adjacent cut edges, utilizing the 5/8" seam allowance.

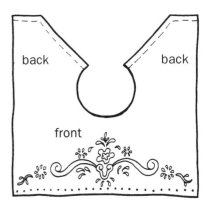

3 Baste collar to garment neckline, both right sides up, matching center fronts. Back collar edges will parallel closure.

back view

4 Continue garment construction. Collar neckline will be finished simultaneously with garment neckline.

Detachable Linen Accents

Although detachable collars and tabards look as if they are part of a garment, they actually extend a garment's usefulness by offering the versatility of an accessory. Detachable techniques are also helpful when the linen and garment do not have identical cleaning requirements. Any of these detachable projects could be permanently attached to the garment, if you prefer.

More than one detachable collar may be designed for a garment or one detachable collar may be used on several garments. In the color photographs you'll see how these three Hankie Collars make one dress suitable for three different holiday occasions.

Upcoming project directions explain how a neck opening plus shoulder seams enable a flat linen to fit a body, while the linen's finished edges eliminate customary construction steps of stitching, turning, and pressing. Some linens have enough weight and stability to eliminate interfacing as well.

Most hankies, however, are thin and not dimensionally stable. Interfacings such as Pellon Sof-Shape or Handler Touch o' Gold provide support without stiffness. Always test interfacings using scraps of similar weight from previous projects or unusable parts of other hankies.

Neckline finishes and closures are usually interchangeable among collar variations. Neckline techniques include shaped facing, bias facing, bias binding, and lining. Closure options include snaps, ties, and buttons with either buttonholes or thread loops.

These collar and tabard projects were designed using complete bodice patterns. (See page 6.) Mark the 5/8"-wide seam allowances on the collar pattern you're making except at neckline. Mark (and later sew) *collar* neck seam allowance at 1/2"-wide to assure that *garment* neck edge (with its standard 5/8"-wide seam allowance) will be concealed when collar is worn.

*"**I** crocheted and knitted my way through college classes—it kept me alert since my fingers were always busy. I could easily drop a crochet hook or knitting needle to take a few notes. I made certain to get an "A" on my first exam so my professor wouldn't mind my needlework. Years later I connected the squares into a finished tablecloth and bedspread that are now heirlooms for my children."*
—Clotilde

Hankie Collars

Although each of the following collars uses only one hankie, notice how the collar style showcases the specific type of hankie embellishment. For instance, the Square Hankie Collar uses a plain hankie with a lace edging, the Diagonal Hankie Collar emphasizes one prominent motif, and the Four Corners Hankie Collar allows all four embellished hankie corners to be admired.

Square Hankie Collar

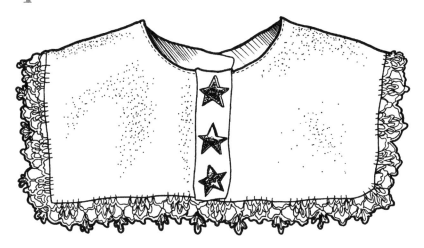

Supplies

- 1 lace-edged hankie
- garment bodice patterns
- approximately 1/2 yard fusible interfacing
- one or more buttons

Procedure

1 Please read introduction to *Detachable Linen Accents* on page 26 and *Using Linens for Apparel* on page 6. Make a complete front bodice pattern, according to page 6.

2 Cut hankie in half, then temporarily mark midpoint of each half.

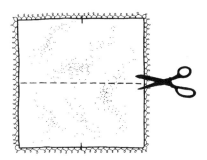

3 Lay one hankie half over bodice front pattern. If hankie width matches pattern width, continue instructions, omitting references to tuck. If hankie is wider than bodice, pin a tuck at hankie midpoint,

until hankie fits inside pattern sleeve seam allowances.

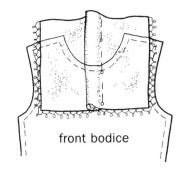

front bodice

4 Sew tuck, then press it flat, matching hankie midpoint to tuck stitching line. Replace pattern and trim hankie along neck and shoulders.

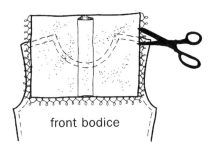

front bodice

5 Cut remaining hankie half in half again.

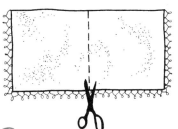

6 Lay these sections right sides together, and pin to bodice back pattern. Check that back collar shoulder seam equals already cut front collar shoulder seam. Trim hankie layers along neck and shoulders. *Do not* trim hankie layers along pattern's center back edge, as this extension will be used for the button and buttonhole.

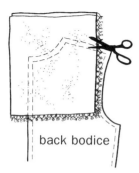

back bodice

7 Sew collar front to backs at shoulder seams, right sides together. Trim seam allowances close to stitching, and press toward front. If the lace edging has large openings, it will not seam together satisfactorily. In this circumstance, separate lace from hankie fabric in seam allowance area. After seaming fabric layers, fold under each bit of loose lace edging at shoulder seams, and secure with either hand stitches or fabric glue.

8 Pin collar to a generously sized piece of fusible interfacing, right sides together. Sew together at center back edges (5/8" seam allowance) and neckline (1/2" seam allowance). For now, cut excess interfacing *only* along sewn edges. Trim seam allowance and corners, clip curves, and understitch.

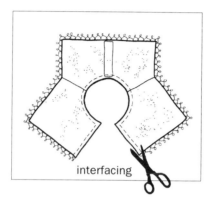

interfacing

9 Turn collar and interfacing right sides out, using point turner to gently nudge corners. Press lightly around sewn edges, then smooth interfacing while gradually pressing almost to collar outer edges. Carefully trim interfacing even with collar edges just before lace edging begins. Then fuse interfacing permanently, according to product directions.

10 Because the interfacing finished only the fabric portion of the collar back edges, the lace edges are still loose. Fold under each lace end and secure with either hand stitches or fabric glue.

11 Sew buttonhole(s) on left collar back and corresponding button(s) on right collar back. If your collar front fits the bodice front without a tuck, there will be no excess fabric to overlap at center back, so substitute a thread loop for the buttonhole.

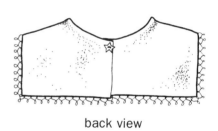

back view

12 Accent center front pleat with buttons, if desired.

*"**W**hen my daughter Rebecca was six, I made her a dress using a hankie for the collar. Her friend observed, "That's handy—if you have a runny nose you can just blow it on the collar!"*
—*Janice Ferguson, teacher, and writer for* **Creative Needle Magazine**

Diagonal Hankie Collar

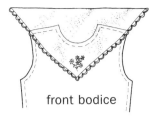

not extend into neck seam allowance.

front bodice

If there is no lace edge to preserve, put both hankie halves together, and trim hemmed edges. Cover cut edges later with lace.

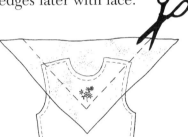

front bodice

Supplies

- 1 hankie with one embellished corner
- enough lace to cover hankie edges if they're plain
- garment bodice patterns
- approximately 1/2 yard fabric for collar, lining, and binding
- approximately 1/4 yard fusible interfacing
- ribbon for trim and/or tie, optional

Procedure

1 Please read introduction to *Detachable Linen Accents* on page 26 and *Using Linens for Apparel* on page 6. Make a complete front bodice pattern according to page 6.

2 Clean and starch hankie. Cut hankie in half diagonally.

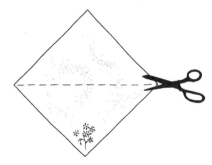

3 Lay the embellished hankie half over bodice front pattern. If hankie edges extend over sleeve seam allowances, there are two solutions. Slide a lace-edged hankie farther up bodice front pattern, as long as embellishment does

4 Replace front bodice pattern on embellished hankie half, and trim hankie along neck and shoulders.

5 Cut reserved hankie half in half again.

6 Lay right sides together and pin to bodice back pattern. Check that back collar shoulder seam equals already cut front collar shoulder seam. Trim

hankie along neck and shoulders.

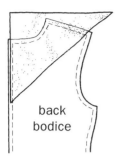

back bodice

7 To make pattern for collar's fabric layer, place collar front on graph paper. Trace neck and shoulder edges. Draw lines to connect the three linen points. Then draw parallel lines 5/8" away, to add seam allowance.

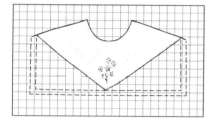

8 Repeat graph paper steps for collar back.

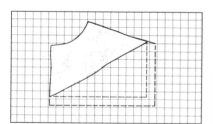

9 Select a companion fabric that either matches or complements hankie. Cut two front fabric layers (one for collar and one for lining) and four back fabric layers (two for collar backs and two for lining). Cut and fuse

interfacing, according to product directions, to fabric collar front and back sections. Sew shoulder seams of interfaced fabric sections and press open, then repeat for lining (non-interfaced) fabric sections. Pin fabric collars right sides together, and sew perimeter seam. *Do not* sew the neck or the back edges.

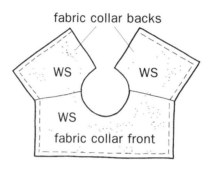

fabric collar backs

WS WS

WS

fabric collar front

10 Trim seam allowance and corners. Turn collar right sides out, using point turner to gently nudge corners, and then press.

11 Sew shoulder seams of hankie collar front and back. Trim close to stitching, and press seam allowances toward front.

12 Pin hankie collar onto fabric collar, both right sides up, aligning centers and shoulder seams.

Narrowly zigzag next to hankie's lace edge, through all thicknesses; or edgestitch lace to cover a plain-edged hankie, folding a tuck in lace at center front point.

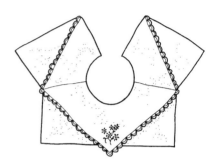

13 To remove neck and back seam allowances for binding, sew around neck 1/2" from edge. Along center back, sew 5/8" from each edge. Then trim close to stitching. Using bias-cut fabric strips, narrowly bind back edges first, and then neck edges. For tie closure, either extend neck binding at center back, or attach ribbon.

back view

Four Corners Hankie Collar

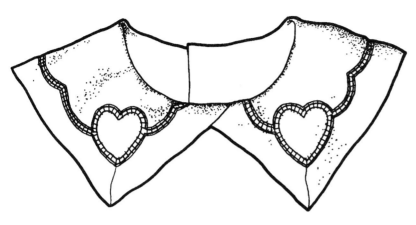

Supplies

- 1 hankie at least 10" square with four embellished corners
- fabric and fusible interfacing scraps for facings
- garment bodice patterns
- 4 snaps
- Res-Q Tape or other double-sided tape

Procedure

1 Please read introduction to *Detachable Linen Accents* on page 26 and *Using Linens for Apparel* on page 6. Make complete front bodice and back bodice patterns, according to page 6.

2 Clean and starch hankie. Cut hankie into equal fourths.

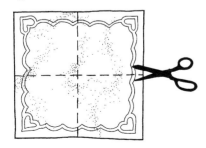

3 Lay two hankie pieces over front bodice pattern, lapping right over left, with edges meeting at center front. Position each lower corner directly below shoulder/neck intersection, and an equal distance from pattern center line. Also check that the cut corners closest to center front extend past neck seam line. Pin hankie pieces to pattern, then trim along neck and shoulders.

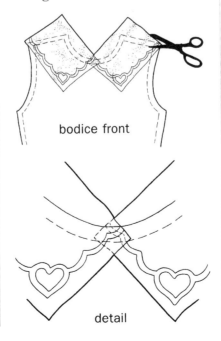

bodice front

detail

4 Remove pattern, keeping fronts pinned together, then baste them together inside neck seam allowance.

5 Pin back bodice patterns together along center back seam. Place remaining hankie pieces over back bodice patterns, lapping left over right, with edges meeting at center back. Position each lower corner equal distance from pattern center line. Check that back collar shoulder seam equals already cut front collar shoulder seam, and that the cut corners closest to center back extend past neck seam line. Pin hankie pieces to pattern, then trim along neck and shoulders.

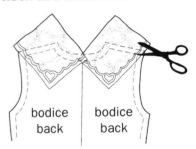

bodice back   bodice back

6 French-seam collar front to backs at shoulders, pressing seam allowances toward front. Fold in and invisibly tack the small corner of seam allowance showing at collar's outside edges.

7 For collar facings, select a fabric similar to hankie. Use pattern's front and back neck facing pieces, but cut a

1" extension over to selvages at center back to allow for back collar overlap.

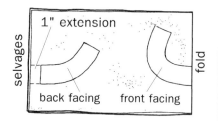

8 Interface facings, sew shoulder seams, and finish facing outer edge. Sew facing to collar, right sides together, matching center front and shoulder seams, using a 1/2"-wide seam allowance. Trim, clip, and understitch seam allowance. Press seam with facing extended—*do not* press facing underneath collar.

9 Lap left back collar over right back collar. Sew snaps on facing edges at back overlap.

back view

10 A few pieces of double-sided fabric tape, such as Res-Q Tape, will temporarily secure collar facing to garment facing during wear. Collar will roll over garment's neck edge.

"My first Affordable Heirloom was a collar I made in a Mildred Turner class using my Grandmother's hankie. I was named after my Grandmother and the hankie is embroidered with our initial E. I've enjoyed wearing something that was part of my heritage."
—Edna Powers

Tea Towel Tabard

Today a tabard is thought of and used as a detachable collar, the only difference being that it's longer and ties at the sides. Please read introduction to *Detachable Linen Accents* on page 26 and *Using Linens for Apparel* on page 6. Make complete front and back bodice patterns, according to page 6.

Supplies

- 1 tea towel
- garment bodice patterns
- approximately 1 yard of 7/8"-wide Seams Great or other lightweight fabric
- fabric scraps or approximately 1-3/4 yards ribbon for ties

Procedure

1 Clean and starch towel. Measure front bodice pattern width between sleeve seam allowances. Trim and hem towel sides, if necessary, to equal bodice width.

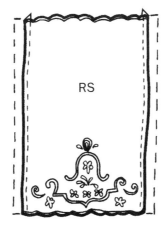

2 Cut towel in half crosswise.

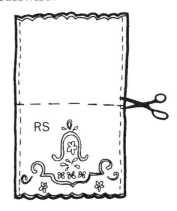

3 Pin front bodice pattern to embellished towel half. (For a high-waisted garment, plan for tabard to be slightly longer than finished bodice.) Trim towel along neck and shoulders.

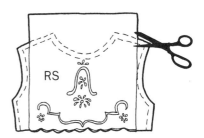

4 Pin back bodice patterns together along center back, then pin to remaining towel half. Check that back collar length equals already cut front collar length. Trim towel along neck and shoulders.

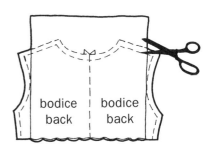

5 Transfer center back marking to collar, down from neck edge for about 6".

6 French-seam collar front to back at shoulders, pressing seam allowances toward front.

7 For a non-bulky, nearly invisible bias facing, finish neckline and back opening using 7/8"-wide Seams Great. Note that this product should not be touched directly with a hot iron, and that when stretched gently, it curls toward its wrong side. (If Seams Great is not available, substitute a lightweight, bias-cut fabric.)

8 Cut a strip of Seams Great longer than back opening. Pin it, right sides together, to tabard's center back marking. Using a short stitch length, sew 1/8" to the left of marked line, pivot and sew two stitches across bottom, then pivot again and sew back to neck edge.

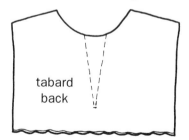

9 Carefully apply seam sealant, such as Fray Check, in between stitching lines. Let dry, and then slash to

pivot point. Turn Seams Great through slit and press from tabard side. Topstitch around opening, then carefully trim Seams Great close to topstitching.

10 Staystitch neckline 3/8" from edge. Right sides together, slightly stretch Seams Great as you sew it to neckline, 1/2" from edge.

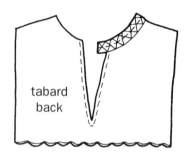

11 Trim, clip, and understitch seam allowance. Fold Seams Great underneath and press from tabard side. Topstitch around neck, then carefully trim Seams Great close to topstitching.

12 Sew button(s) to the right side of neck opening and thread loop(s) to the left side of neck opening.

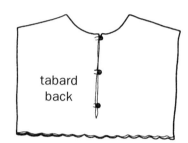

13 Attach four 15"-long ribbons or fabric ties to tabard's four lower corners.

"I searched for weeks to find the perfect floral print to enhance but not dominate the exquisite embroidery on this tea towel. The best choice turned out to be a simple blue and white gingham. The tabard ties are gingham, as well."
—Gaye Kriegel

Embellishing Ready-to-Wear

The linens are already embellished and the garments are already made. All you do is have fun combining them? This is too good to be true.

The one and only rule of embellishing ready-made clothes is that for cleaning purposes the embellishment must be compatible or removable. Temporary connections for embellishments include buttons, button pins, safety pins, hook-and-loop tape, ties, pressure-sensitive glue, and snaps.

1 *What do you embellish?* Raid your husband's closet—with permission, of course—or bargain hunt at resale shops and garage sales for jackets, vests, and more. Check garments carefully since purchases are usually final.

2 *What do you embellish with?* Virtually any linen (or piece of linen), including hankies, napkins, dresser scarves, hot roll covers, and doilies of any size, shape, or style. And certainly don't forget buttons, jewelry, lace, and other trims.

3 *Where do you embellish?* Study the design of the garment, and then select embellishments to highlight and enhance a collar, cuff, lapel, yoke, seam, band, welt pocket, patch pocket, or pocket flap. Your embellishments may have a common element or not, have symmetrical placement or not, be limited to small amounts or not.

Rearrange embellishments to your heart's content, then pin everything in place. Before finalizing your decisions, try on garment, to avoid embarrassing or unflattering surprises.

4 *How do you embellish?* Some embellishments may be glued or machine-sewn, but since the garment is already assembled, many embellishments look better and are easier to apply when hand-sewn. Don't groan; just put up your feet, listen to television or music, and enjoy the process. Choose thread color to match embellishment.

Utilize a linen's finished edges whenever possible, or fold cut edges under before sewing. Turned-under edges can be shaped around a curve if linen edges are clipped first. Sew or glue trims to cover folded edges, if desired.

Never assume that square garment sections are actually square, or that a garment's left and right sides measure equally. Custom-fit each linen piece that you add.

"I'm making a business from decorating jackets and vests with customers' family mementos, but, more importantly, I'm making memories for them."—B. J. Tichinin

Since ready-to-wear garments are not always ready to wear, here are a few situations and possible solutions.

1 *The jacket sleeves are too long.* You *could* hem them, but then again, you could just roll them up and let the lining show.

2 *The jacket shoulders are too wide.* Add more shoulder pads or wear shoulder pads under your blouse. Revel at how narrow your hips will look. Or try the Blind-stitched Tuck as mentioned on page 54 of *Innovative Sewing.* (See Bibliography, page 114.)

3 *The buttons are missing or ugly.* Change them. Choose a matching set or an assortment, new or old, subtle or stunning.

4 *The jacket or vest is too big in the waist.* Let it be. Or add a brace across the back, making it part of your embellishment, if you want. Or create an elastic casing between side seams with two rows of topstitching that join garment back and lining together. Open a few lining stitches at each casing end, insert elastic, and secure elastic by topstitching in side seams.

5 *Your linen will cover a garment buttonhole.* Temporarily pin linen on garment to accurately mark buttonhole location onto linen. Remove linen, pin interfacing scrap under mark, machine-sew buttonhole, and slit open. Reposition linen on garment, tacking buttonhole layers together, if desired. Button through holes simultaneously.

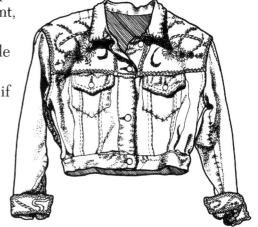

Part II
Accessories

These accessories do for you what all accessories should—add versatility to your wardrobe, with only small investments of time and materials. Whether your style is casual, tailored, romantic, or a bit of each, there's an accessory to match your every mood.

"When I tell people that I like buttons, the first thing they're reminded of is a particular button box. 'My grandmother (mother, aunt, or the lady down the street) let me play with her button box.' Many remember a round tin box and the sound the buttons made when they shook it, or a see-through button jar that glowed with a jumble of color. Some remember the smell. My grandmother's button box smelled (and still smells) like a mixture of plastic, sachet powder, and tailor's chalk."
—Marilyn Green, author, The Button Lover's Book

Jewelry

The Doily Pin and the Recycled Jewelry Pin offer perfect excuses to sift through your button and jewelry boxes. They are equally appropriate on a silk dress, denim jacket, or wool suit lapel. Depending on the embellishment, the Heart's Desire Pendant and Covered Button Earrings could complement any garment, from a dress to a sweatshirt.

Doily Pin ✂

A few simple folds and some old buttons combine to make an easy but elegant pin.

Supplies

- 1 round doily, 5"–6" diameter
- approximately 6–10 assorted old buttons
- other optional embellishments, such as charms, ribbons, lace snippets
- hand needle, thread, scissors
- .015"-thick plastic styrene sheet or recycled plastic coffee can lid
- jewelry glue, such as E6000
- pin back
- permanent pen such as Identipen, optional (available at office supply stores)

Procedure

1 Wash and press doily, if needed. Fold doily as follows, positioning a specific design in center of top layer, if desired. Our project doily was embroidered with one large and three small designs.

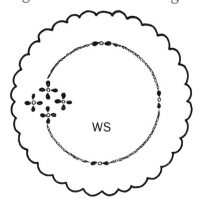

2 Fold doily in half in between motifs, wrong sides together.

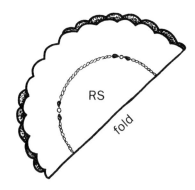

3 Then fold in half again, and design will be centered on top layer. Secure layers together with a few hand or machine stitches. *Do not press the folds*—their rounded edges enhance the pin's depth.

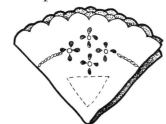

4 The buttons will be stacked at the doily's folded point. Plan button arrangement by positioning largest buttons on lowest layer, reserving smaller, more decorative buttons for upper layers. Somewhat damaged buttons may be used on first layer, and then partially concealed by another button. A few buttons may extend slightly past doily's folded edges and still be sufficiently supported.

5 A shank button is a bit harder to work with because it doesn't stack flat. Remove shank (with jewelry nippers or wire cutters—not your scissors), or simply nestle shank between two other buttons.

6 Hand-sew or glue buttons or other embellishments onto pointed end of folded doily. Although the first button layer may be sewn on, upper button layers must be glued, since the needle is blocked by the buttons underneath. If you want an upper button to look as if it were sewn on, sew through its holes, knot thread under button, and then glue it in place. Filling a button's holes with thread also helps prevent glue from oozing through.

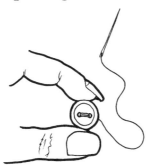

7 Trace pin backing pattern below. Check to be sure the support will be concealed behind folded doily. Cut pattern shape from plastic sheet, or, if you prefer to recycle, the plastic lid from a coffee can. Glue backing underneath doily.

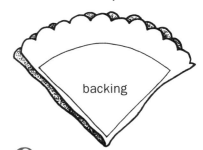

8 Glue a pin back near top edge of backing. (If pin back is positioned too low, the pin will flop forward during wear.) Let dry thoroughly. For a nice added touch, sign and date the backing, using a permanent pen.

See pattern below.

Doily Pin Pattern

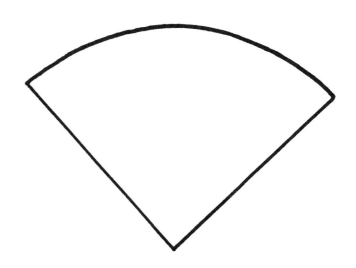

Recycled Jewelry Pin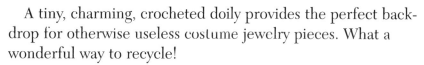

A tiny, charming, crocheted doily provides the perfect backdrop for otherwise useless costume jewelry pieces. What a wonderful way to recycle!

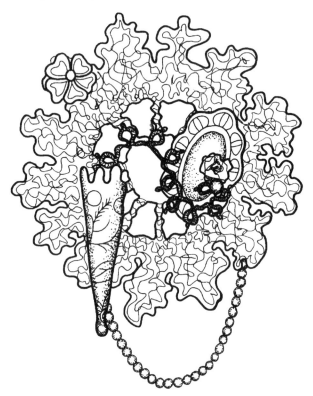

Supplies

- 2" diameter crocheted doily
- .015"-thick clear plastic styrene sheet
- jewelry glue, such as E6000
- assorted jewelry pieces
- jewelry nippers or wire cutters
- pin back
- permanent pen such as Identipen, optional (available at office supply stores)

Procedure

1 Cut backing from plastic sheet, trying to have its edge concealed behind a ring of the crochet. Spread glue on wrong side of doily, and attach backing.

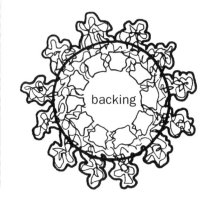

2 Glue assorted jewelry pieces to doily front. For example, our project has a pin whose chipped porcelain flower is covered with a scrap of tatting. Orphaned pierced earring (with post cut off) and bolo tie end complement the flower pin, while a section of a broken pearl bracelet dangles below.

3 Glue a pin back near top edge of backing. (If pin back is positioned too low, the pin will flop forward during wear.) Let dry thoroughly. Use a permanent pen to sign and date plastic support, if desired.

"My mother-in-law, Esther, saved everything. I assembled this pin from broken and orphaned pieces of her costume jewelry. The crocheted doily was in her box of laces that had been carefully removed from worn-out clothes."
—Gaye Kriegel

Heart's Desire Pendant

Designed to showcase small pieces of linens, this pendant is padded on the front only, so that it lays flat against the body. If you prefer a pin to the pendant, simply substitute a pin back instead of the cord. Reduce the pattern to make matching earrings, if desired.

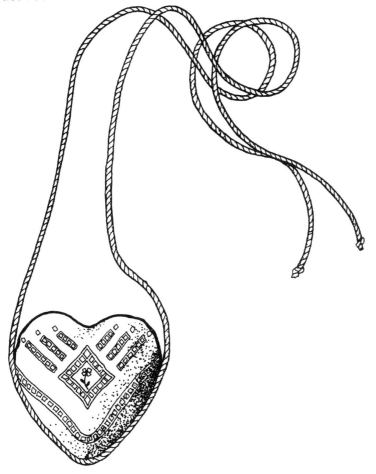

Supplies

- pattern paper and pencil
- pieces of hankie or other lightweight linen with embellished corner(s)
- seam sealant, such as Fray-Check
- small piece of cardboard, such as recycled tablet backing
- felt or synthetic suede scrap for backing
- small pieces of fleece
- fast-drying white glue, such as Aleene's Designer "Tacky" Glue
- flat toothpicks, helpful
- hand needle and thread, optional
- wax paper
- books for weight
- 1 to 1-1/2 yards narrow decorative cord

Procedure

1 Trace heart-shaped fabric cover pattern (including slash line and point) and cardboard pattern both from page 42.

2 Measure 3" down each side from hankie's embellished corner, and cut off corner diagonally. Lay corner over remaining larger solid section of hankie, both right sides up, and topstitch together with narrow zigzag along corner's two finished edges.

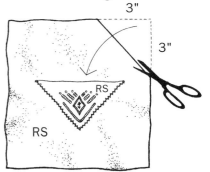

3 Center cover pattern over pieced fabric, trace around, and then cut. Slash along dotted line to point. Coat slash and fabric perimeter with seam sealant, and set aside to dry.

4 Trace cardboard pattern onto both cardboard and felt backing. Cut each one, trimming felt backing 1/8" smaller.

5 Cut the following fleece layers: two the same size as cardboard, two smaller than cardboard, and one larger than cardboard (but smaller than the fabric cover). Slash top of largest fleece on dotted line.

6 Layer progressively larger fleece pieces on top of cardboard. Turn stack over, use toothpick to apply glue on cardboard's perimeter. Then wrap largest fleece layer to back, and let dry.

7 With right side up, sew around near edge of fabric cover by hand or machine, beginning and ending at top slash. Temporarily tape top threads to cover front (to prevent tangling) as you pull each bobbin thread, gathering fullness. Insert cardboard, padded side toward cover. Pull bobbin threads tightly, distribute gathers, and tie all threads together.

8 Glue cover edges to cardboard. Then glue backing fabric to conceal cover's cut edges. Set on waxed paper, weigh down with books, and let dry.

9 Tie overhand knots in cord ends, to prevent raveling. Match midpoint of cord to bottom of heart. Glue or hand-sew cord around lower two-thirds of pendant.

See pattern below.

Heart's Desire Pendant Pattern

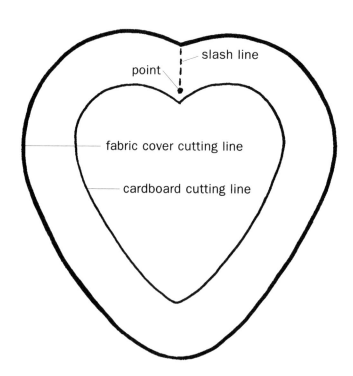

slash line

point

fabric cover cutting line

cardboard cutting line

Covered Button Earrings

Waste not, want not—tiny bits of embroidery are salvaged and shown beautifully on their own, or made to match other *Affordable Heirlooms* accessories.

Supplies

- two 5/8"-diameter half-ball buttons-to-cover, such as Dritz brand kit containing rubber mold
- needle-nose pliers
- 2 small pieces of embellished linen
- white lining scrap
- pierced earring posts
- jewelry glue, such as E6000
- for optional dangle: 4 tiny buttons, 2 jump rings, and 3" of fine-gauge chain

Procedure

1 Use needle-nose pliers to pull off shank from button backs.

2 Lay linen piece right side down over rubber button mold, centering design, if any. Layer a small circle of white lining fabric, and then button shell, on linen piece. (The lining helps prevent the shine of the metal shell from showing through.)

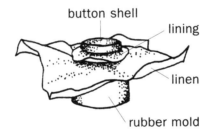

3 Press layers into mold. Trim excess linen before folding its edges into shell center. Dot altered button back with glue and press on. Remove from mold and repeat for other button. Glue earring posts at uppermost edge of button backs.

4 Add a quick, optional dangle to your Covered Button Earring by gluing two tiny buttons back-to-back, with a 1-1/2" long fine-gauge chain in between. Attach a small jump ring on the opposite chain end, to slip over earring post. Repeat steps for other dangle.

Since the dangle is not permanently attached, wear it only when you want to. If desired, make more than one pair of dangles, in different lengths with different button sizes but still proportionately smaller than covered button earring.

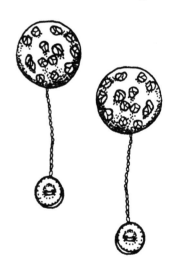

A Victorian Touch ✄

Our varied lives require clothing from casual to business to dressy. Since these quick projects are equally as appropriate for denim as for silk, you can use them to add just a touch of Victorian charm to any style of garment.

Cuff Ruffle ✄

2 Pin elastic to right side of doily, 1" above center, matching end marks and midpoint of elastic to sides and midpoint of doily. Since doily is longer than elastic, excess doily will bunch up in between pins.

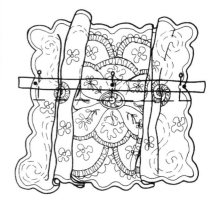

3 Set machine for short, narrow zigzag. Backstitch to secure stitching, and then sink needle. Use one hand to hold elastic "handle" behind presser foot while the other hand grasps the doily and elastic at midpoint. Stretch elastic, sew to midpoint, and sink needle. Again grasp elastic behind presser foot and opposite elastic end; stretch elastic,

Supplies

- 2 lace doilies, approximately 9" x 13"
- approximately 20" of 3/8"-wide clear elastic, such as Lastin

Procedure

1 Wrap elastic around forearm where cuff will be worn, pulling until snug but still comfortable. Pinch elastic at finished size, slip off hand, and mark pinch with pencil. Also mark midway between end marks. Trim elastic 1" beyond each end mark, to allow for "handles." Cut and mark a duplicate elastic piece for other cuff.

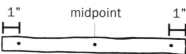

1"   midpoint   1"

sew to doily edge, and back-stitch. Trim excess elastic from ends.

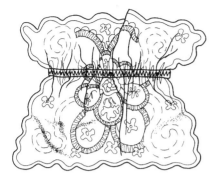

4 Fold narrower part of doily over elastic. Match short edges, and topstitch through all thicknesses either part of the way or completely down the side. Repeat for other cuff.

Topstitch.

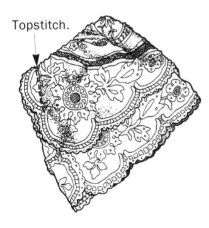

Slip cuffs onto forearms, under jacket sleeves, showing as much or as little ruffle as you prefer. (Yes, you have to leave your jacket on.)

Scarf ✂

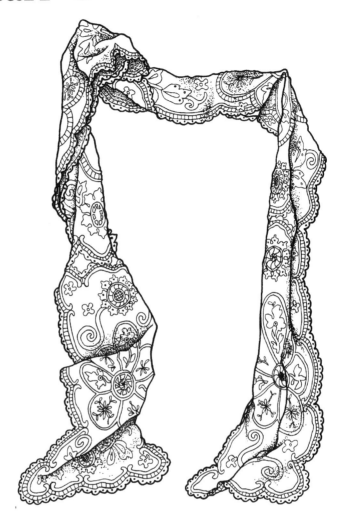

Supplies

- 5 rectangular lace doilies, approximately 5" x 12"
- hand needle and thread

Procedure

Slightly overlap and pin together the short ends of doilies. Tack ends together using a few hand stitches.

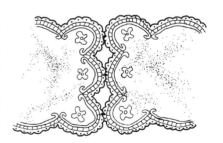

Scarf is perfect to wear under jacket lapels or over a sweater.

Faux Bow ✄

Supplies

- 1 embellished hankie, approximately 11" square
- approximately 24" of 1/2"-wide ribbon
- hand needle and thread
- 1 snap

Procedure

1 Sew a gathering thread vertically through midpoint of hankie.

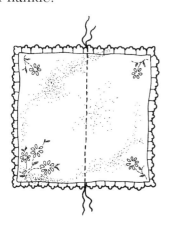

2 Gather tightly by pulling up bobbin threads at each end. Knot with top threads to secure gathers.

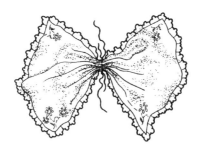

3 Cut a 2-1/2" piece of ribbon. Loop it around hankie gathers; turn under one ribbon end, and pin it over other end, without catching hankie. Slide remaining ribbon under pinned loop until middle of ribbon is under loop. Hand-sew loop ends together, securing ribbon piece underneath and also securing hankie to prevent it from slipping out of loop.

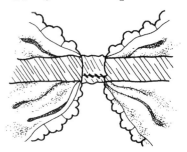

4 Slip ribbon under garment's collar, to check finished length. Cut each end of neck ribbon 1-1/4" longer than finished length. Fold under 1/2" twice at each end; then sew on snaps, simultaneously securing folds.

Jabot ✂

point through all thicknesses, to secure layers and to reduce bulk.

4 Sew button on front side of jabot pivot point. Glue button cover to back side of pivot point, weigh down with books, and let dry thoroughly. To wear, slip button cover over shirt's button.

Supplies

- crocheted doily, approximately 10" in diameter
- hand needle and thread
- button cover
- 1 non-shank button, larger than diameter of button cover
- jewelry glue, such as E6000
- books for weight

Procedure

1 Fold doily almost in half, wrong sides together.

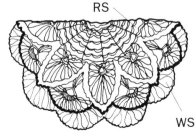

RS

WS

2 Mark a pivot point 1" left of center, and visually divide doily into three increasingly larger sections.

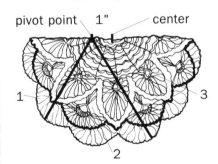

pivot point   1"   center

1

3

2

3 Pinching the pivot point, fold sections two and three towards the left under section one. Then fold section three back to the right under sections one and two. The progressively larger sections create a cascade effect. Sew several stitches near pivot

Top That

What better way to top off an outfit than with custom-made hair accessories or hats, which are fun for all ages? When you've sewn a garment, extra fabrics, linens, laces, ribbons, or buttons can be incorporated into the accessories. Remember that a too-large accessory may overpower a small child, so keep designs in proportion.

Use a Doily Bow or Doily Flower to embellish a metal barrette, plastic or padded headband, fabric-covered elastic headband, hat, or for that matter, a purse, pin back, or shoe clip.

Don't give away the secret, but the beautiful Padded Headband is nothing more than a few simple scraps covering an inexpensive plastic headband.

Doily Bow ✂

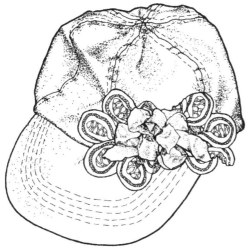

Supplies

- 3"-6" diameter doily
- hand needle and thread
- accent, as described below
- paper, pencil, compass, and fabric scrap for optional backing

Procedure

1 Use your fingers to make small pleats across the doily's center, beginning and ending with the doily edge turned to the underside.

Secure pleats using a hand needle and a double strand of thread.

2 The decorative accent you choose to sew or glue to the bow's center will conceal your stitches. Options

include one or more ribbon bows, silk flowers, buttons, charms, fabric strip, cord, or any combination of these.

3 A fabric backing is another way to enhance the Doily Bow. Lay flat doily on a piece of paper. Setting a compass point in center of doily, trace a circle that is 1/2"-3/4" larger than doily all around.

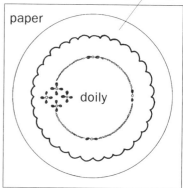

1/2" to 3/4" larger

paper

doily

4 Use this paper pattern to cut two fabric layers. Sew fabric circles, right sides together, with a 1/4"-wide seam allowance. Pink or notch seam allowance. Cut a slit in the middle of *one* fabric circle.

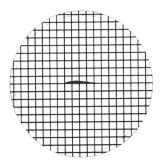

5 Turn circle right sides out through the slit, and press flat. Position fabric circle under wrong side of doily; baste through all thicknesses where you plan to pleat. (Fabric slit will be concealed in pleats.) Continue steps as directed above.

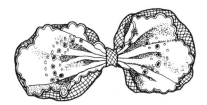

6 Sew or glue the Doily Bow embellishment to the accessory of your choice.

Doily Flower ✂

Supplies

- 3"-6" diameter doily
- small rubber band
- hand needle and thread, optional
- accent, optional

Procedure

1 Hold doily in one hand. Push center of embroidered side of doily against extended index finger of the other hand. Compress and cinch doily around finger. Slide your finger out of doily securing the cinch with a small rubber band. (The farther onto your finger that the doily is cinched, the smaller the Doily Flower.) Adjust gathers as necessary.

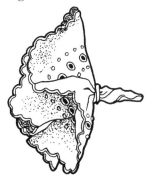

2 Conceal center of doily behind Doily Flower. Tack, if desired.

3 If excess doily behind Doily Flower is too bulky, instead of using a rubber band, sew a few stitches by hand, wrap thread around doily to secure gathers, then knot thread. Cut off excess doily close to stitches. Then obviously, you will no longer have a no-cut project.

4 If desired, accent center with ribbon bows, silk flowers, or buttons. Use Doily Flowers in the same ways as Doily Bows, described earlier.

Padded Headband

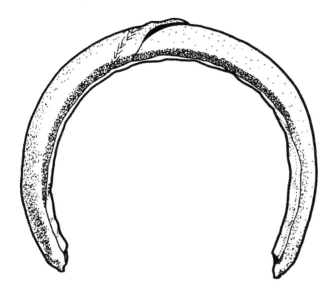

Supplies

- plastic headband, 1/2"-1" wide
- paper and pencil
- fleece scrap(s)
- linen scrap(s)
- white glue
- scissors, hand needle, and thread
- felt strip or ribbon

Procedure

1 Set one end of headband on a strip of paper, and trace around it. Rotate headband a little at a time, continuing to trace it, as the center and then the opposite end touch the paper.

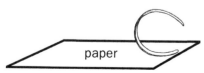

paper

2 Set headband aside, and straighten your drawn lines, if necessary.

3 Cut a strip of fleece as long as pattern and 1/4" wider than pattern on each side.

4 The fabric cover must be cut on the bias grain, in order to smooth over fleece without puckers. Cut cover from linen scrap 1/4" bigger than fleece all around.

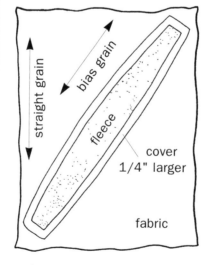

straight grain

bias grain

fleece

cover 1/4" larger

fabric

5 If you do not have a linen scrap large enough to cut cover in one piece, lap hemmed edge of one scrap over cut edge of another scrap (as many times as necessary) to get a large enough piece. Secure scraps with topstitching.

6 Run a line of glue along the upper side of headband. Glue fleece strip to it and let dry. Prepare needle with a double strand of thread. Lay band, fleece side down, onto wrong side of cover. Beginning at band's center, wrap cover edges to band's underside. It doesn't matter if cover edges gap, meet, or overlap. Sew back and forth between cover's edges.

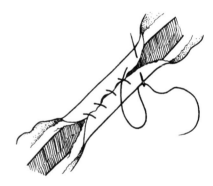

7 As you wrap and stitch toward one band end (and then from the center to the other end), fold cover under at ends before you fold sides. Trim excess bulk, if necessary.

8 Conceal stitches and fabric raw edges by gluing on a ribbon or a felt strip.

Part III

Gifts

Whether you are continuing a tradition or beginning one, the uniqueness of a linen gift says to the recipient, "You are special." Although you may vary these projects to suit many occasions, they will always be memorable, because a gift from your hands is a gift from your heart.

"As a child in Lebanon my grandmother Emily learned how to make needle lace using only a regular hand needle and ordinary thread. She made yards and yards of this needle lace which she gave to me as gifts. Although she apologized that her gifts were not store-bought, I assured her that I treasured her hand-made lace more than anything she could buy. As she aged, her often trembling hands always steadied when she picked up her needle and thread."
—Carol Ahles, *writes for* Creative Needle Magazine *and is working on a book about fine sewing.*

Christmas Ornaments

Make a memory for your own family at Christmas, or for someone else special. A variety of old or new doilies, hankies, and cocktail napkins is used, plus a few additional supplies, depending on the ornament. Some projects are so simple, they are easily accomplished by a child.

A hanger for each ornament is made from approximately 8" of satin ribbon. Either slip the ribbon through an opening in the linen's lace edging, and then tie ends in an overhand knot, or tie the knot first, and then tack the ribbon's knot or loop to the ornament.

Linens may be further enhanced with hand or machine embroidery—a Christmas design, or perhaps a name and the year. Another option would be to add an embellishment, such as flowers, holly leaves, or a ribbon rosette, where the hanger attaches to the ornament.

Treasure Envelopes, page 64, may also be used for Christmas ornaments.

Snowflake

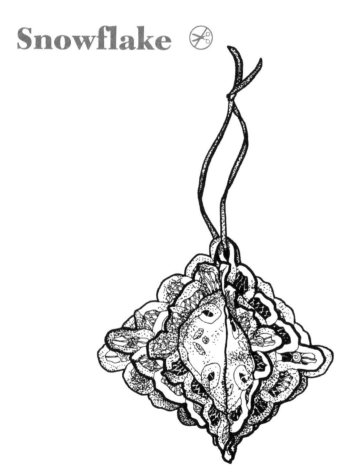

doilies. Sew all doilies together diagonally between two corners.

2 Separate all the layers to form a six-sided snowflake. If you prefer a three-sided snowflake, tack outside corner points of doilies wrong sides together.

3 Attach hanger, as noted earlier.

Procedure

1 Select three identical 4" square doilies. Hold the first two doilies right sides together. Position wrong side of the third doily to wrong side of either of the first two

Affordable Heirlooms

Christmas Ball ✄

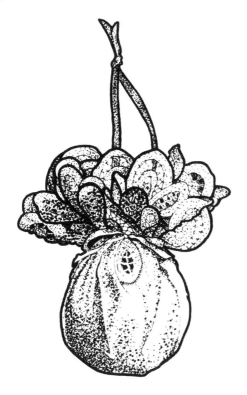

Procedure

1 Select a doily or hankie about 8" in diameter. Wrap linen, right side out, around any ball form you prefer: Styrofoam, plastic, fiberfill, or even a recycled ball ornament.

2 Gather linen at top of form, and tie with an 18" length of ribbon.

3 Attach hanger in center of gathers, as noted above.

Variation

- To show off crochet, cut-work, or other embroidered openings in your linen, choose a form of a contrasting color, such as a red satin ball. Or as you wrap the ball, layer a fabric of a contrasting color as a lining between ball and linen. Cut lining smaller than linen, so that lining edges are covered at the top gathers.

Halo ✄

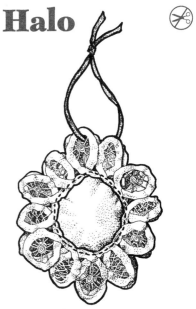

Procedure

1 Place two identical 4"-diameter doilies wrong sides together. Pin nearly all the way around the center fabric section. To add dimension to the center, lightly stuff fiberfill into opening.

2 Close the opening with a pin, and then sew around the center fabric section.

3 Attach hanger, as noted earlier.

Variations

- Use a decorative stitch to attach doilies to each other.
- Omit fiberfill, if desired.
- Fill center with non-oil potpourri
- Use only one doily; then pin felt behind center fabric section before stuffing with fiberfill and sewing together.

Stocking

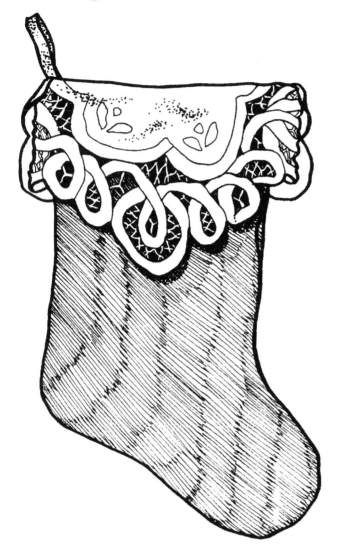

2 Cut a 6"-diameter round doily in half. Pin the right side of each doily half to wrong side of each stocking half, having raw edges even. The lace edges of the doily will overlap each other at stocking side seam lines. Sew or serge around top edge.

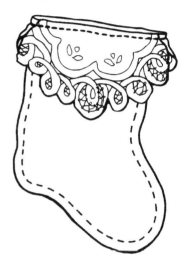

3 Turn stocking right side out, and press flat. Press doily cuff over stocking, covering the seam allowance. Tack cuff, if necessary, to keep edges in position.

4 Attach hanger to stocking's upper center back edge, as noted on page 52.

See pattern next page.

Procedure

1 Cut two pieces of fabric, using stocking pattern on page 55. Red velvet or small Christmas prints look especially nice. With stocking fabric pieces right sides together, sew or serge a

1/4"-wide seam, leaving top edge open.

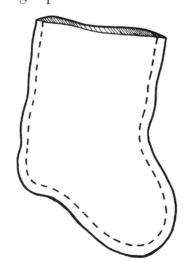

2 *detail of V-Neck Collar*

1 V-Neck Collar, p. 24
Padded Headband, p. 50

5 *Right: Diagonal Hankie Collar, p. 29*

6 *Below left: Square Hankie Collar, p. 27*

7 *Below right: Four Corners Hankie Collar, p. 31*

5–7 *Doily Bow, p. 48*

11 *Embellishing Ready-To-Wear, p. 35; Covered Button Earrings, p. 43; Pillowcase Petticoat, p. 12; Shirt Collar and Pocket Top, p. 20; Doily Flower, p. 49; Tea Towel Tabard, p. 33; Tea Towel Doll, p. 62*

13 *Pillows: Pillowcase, p. 100; Button Edge, p. 98;*
Wrapped Hankie, p. 90; Scrunched Hankie, p. 90;
One-Corner Hankie, p. 89; Collage, p. 92;
Victorian Heart, p. 94

Left: Linen
Silhouette, p. 109

Right: Framed
Hankie, p. 108

Stocking Ornament Pattern

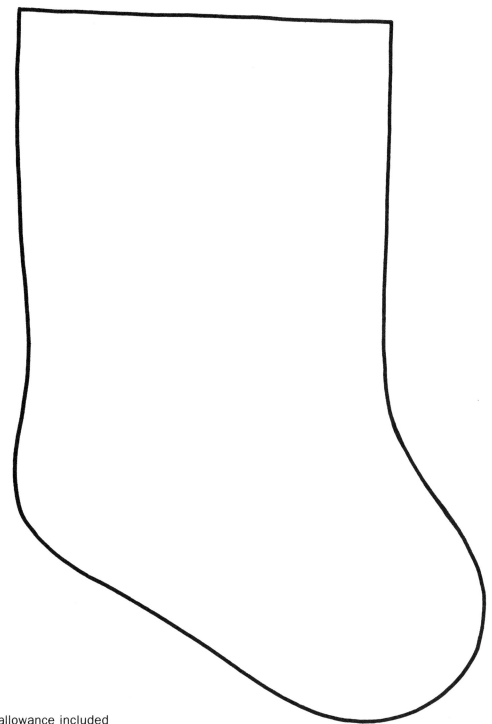

1/4" seam allowance included

Angel ✂

3 Bring linen up and around fiberfill, and secure tightly with about 12" of ribbon, tied in a bow. Or secure with tiny rubber band first and then tie with ribbon.

4 Pull upper napkin corner behind angel's head, and tack or glue. Pull out and crease side corners, to form wings. Fold under and crease fabric on each side of lower corner, to suggest a dress. Tack these creases, if desired.

5 Attach hanger to upper corner, as noted earlier.

Variations

- Glue straw, moss, or purchased doll hair to angel's head.
- A small, starched hankie may substitute for the napkin by slightly increasing amount of fiberfill for head and using a longer length of ribbon.

Procedure

1 Temporarily mark the center of a 6" square, starched napkin. If desired, embroider or paint eyes and a mouth, positioning the mouth in napkin's center.

2 For the angel's head, pull off about 2" of fiberfill. Compress and form it into a smaller, smooth ball, and place it just above the

center mark on linen's wrong side.

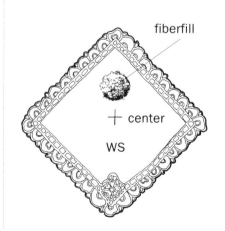

Gifts for Little Ones

If it's true that children learn what they live, then perhaps an *Affordable Heirlooms* gift given at an early age will generate a lifetime appreciation of needlearts.

The Hankie Bonnet and Baby Bottle Cover are sure to receive oohs and aahs at the baby shower. The new mother will appreciate that either gift could once again be a plain hankie to be used another way, if desired.

Purposely simple and certain never to be advertised on a Saturday morning cartoon, either the Tea Towel Teddy or Tea Towel Doll could years from now inspire the reminiscence, "When I was a child, this was my favorite toy."

Hankie Bonnet

A single hankie (new, or already a family heirloom) is easily shaped into an adorable baby bonnet, then just as easily back into a hankie, to be carried in the future by a bride. A time-honored tradition, the hankie bonnet is always a welcomed gift, especially accompanied by a copy of this poem.

Presented at birth
Treasured until marriage
To be carried by the bride or
Given to her by the groom
On their special day.

Author Unknown

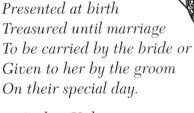

Supplies

- 1 embellished hankie, approximately 12" square
- 3-1/2 yards 1/8"-wide double-sided satin ribbon
- pins, hand needle, thread

Procedure

1 Position hankie, wrong side up, with embellished corner at top. Locate hankie fold lines that follow by measuring from top and bottom corner tips diagonally toward center. (Adjust measurements slightly for a larger or smaller hankie.) To establish bonnet front, fold and pin embellished corner 4-3/4" toward hankie's center.

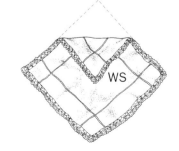

2 To establish bonnet back, fold opposite corner 5-1/2" toward center; then back on itself 2". Tuck second fold under embellished corner, and pin.

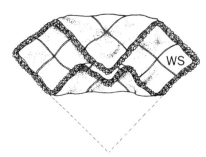

3 Fold each side corner 2" toward center and pin.

4 Secure the four corners with hand stitches. Cut an 18" length of ribbon, and slip it into the back fold.

5 Pull ribbon ends tightly to gather hankie, and then tie ribbon into a bow.

6 Traditionally, bonnets are presented to the recipient with continuous tie ends, which are then clipped apart at the first wearing. To make the continuous tie ends, cut the remaining three yards of ribbon into two, 1-1/2 yard lengths. Tie the two ribbon lengths together in a bow at each end.

7 Tack one bow to each bonnet side, by hand.

*"**M**y mother crocheted the edging on this hankie and many others, because at the time proper young ladies wore a hat and gloves and carried a hankie to accessorize every outfit."*
—*Joann Collins*

Baby Bottle Cover ✂

Sew this unique shower gift or package topper for the baby who has everything. This quick and simple hankie bottle cover may be disassembled later for another use, if desired.

Supplies

- 1 embellished hankie, approximately 11" square
- 12 inches of beading (trim with embroidered openings to hold ribbon)
- 7/8 yard satin ribbon to fit beading openings
- 1 baby bottle

Procedure

1 Designate one hankie edge to be the top. Turning under the cut ends of beading trim (to prevent raveling), pin trim to hankie, both right sides up, about 2" down from hankie's top edge. Edgestitch each long side of trim to hankie.

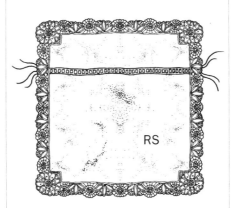

2 Fold hankie in half, right sides together, perpendicular to the trim. Lay folded hankie next to baby bottle, to measure and pin cover's finished length. The top of hankie's lace should just reach bottle's cap. Sew a seam across hankie bottom, along pins. Do not trim seam if you prefer to keep hankie intact.

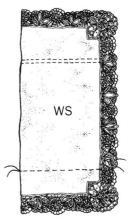

3 Turn hankie right side out. Topstitch cover sides together along lace edging between trim and cover bottom. (Cover will be wider than bottle circumference.)

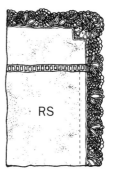

4 Weave ribbon through trim. Place baby bottle inside cover. Pull ribbon ends to tighten, and then tie in a bow.

Tea Towel Teddy

A simple towel makes a simply wonderful teddy bear, who is sure to be a well-loved addition to any family. Other animals besides bears are equally as charming when made of linens. If one linen is not sufficient, sew several together patchwork-style.

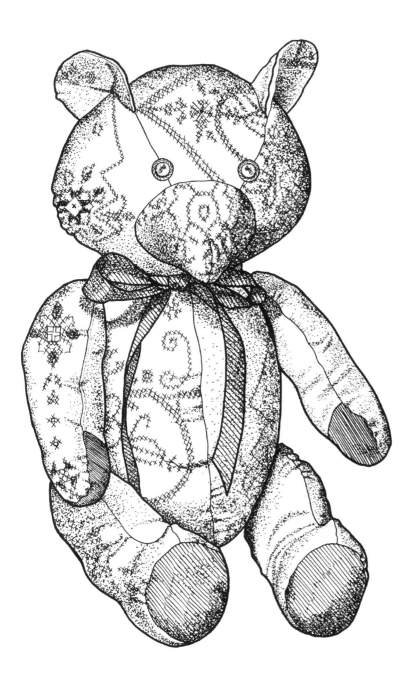

Supplies

- embroidered tea towel, approximately 32" square
- commercial teddy bear pattern
- additional items, such as fiberfill, as noted on pattern
- underlining may be needed to stabilize towel fabric, which may be somewhat thin and transparent (Omit underlining if you're sure seam allowances and stuffing won't show through.)

Procedure

1 Clean, press, and starch tea towel. Prewash and dry underlining fabric.

2 To better decide how to cut towel, select appropriate pattern pieces, and trim off excess tissue margins. Read through the pattern's guide sheet to understand how pieces fit together. Draw arrows on each piece to show the direction it will be on the finished project. Label key seams, such as center front, side seam, head-joins-body, ear-joins-head. Note which pieces are to be cut once, twice, and so on.

3 Lay towel in a single layer, right sides up. Position pattern pieces, taking best advantage of towel's embellishment, disregarding pattern's grainline arrows.

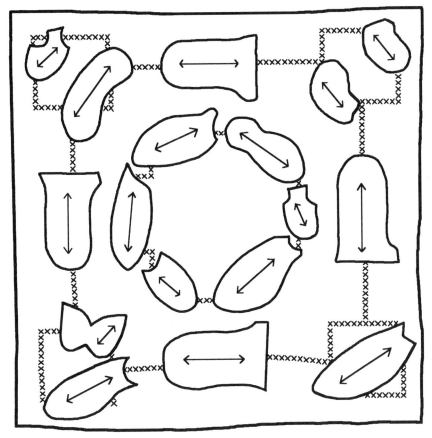

The layout for your pattern and towel will differ but this is how we tried to make the best use of the embellishment.

Transfer pattern markings, if any, to wrong side of underlining. Match each underlining piece to wrong side of corresponding towel piece, then handle each as one unit.

9 Assemble and stuff bear with fiberfill, according to pattern instructions. Give her a name and a hug.

(The seams of our project that were cut with at least a partial bias grain looked better than seams cut on straight grain.)

4 First decide where to place the most important pieces, such as body front and head front. The least important pieces, such as under arm or inner leg, should be cut last, from non-embroidered towel sections, if necessary. If embroidery motifs are a variety of sizes, choose largest motifs for largest pattern pieces.

5 For pattern pieces marked "cut two," remember that to achieve a left and a right while cutting on a single layer of fabric, you must turn the pattern piece over when you cut it the second time.

6 Decide whether you want any pieces to have symmetrical embroidery. Sample project has the same embroidery on each arm and each leg, but all other pieces were cut randomly.

7 Cut, remove pattern pieces, and set cut towel sections aside.

8 Fold underlining fabric, right sides together, and cut all pattern pieces again.

"I've collected more old linens than I could possibly use in this lifetime. Could I send a box of linens for you to look through?"—Carla Lopez

(At least a dozen of the linens bought from Carla were made into Affordable Heirlooms projects.)

Tea Towel Doll ✂

She's charming enough to enchant a child, yet simple enough to inspire imagination—that's what you'll discover, when you make a Tea Towel Doll. Embellishment options allow you to decide just how much personality to add. Since only one towel is used to form the doll and her dress, note that towel color is doll's face color. And one more note: batteries are *not* included.

Supplies

- 1 embellished tea towel
- approximately 3"-diameter ball of fiberfill
- small rubber band

- 1 yard, 1/8"- to 1/4"-wide ribbon for neck tie and bow
- optional embellishments, as noted below

Procedure

1 Locate placement for doll's eyes midway between towel's sides, and 4" down from top hemmed edge.

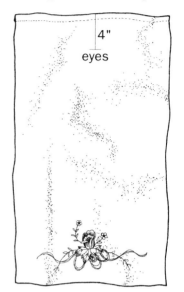

2 Create facial features with embroidery, fabric pens, or objects, such as buttons. Face may be completed while towel is flat, unless you have chosen doll glasses, in which case you will tack glasses to the already-formed head, and space eyes to fit under glasses.

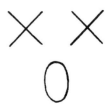

3 Place smoothed and compressed fiberfill ball behind doll's face. Fold towel's upper edge over fiberfill ball, and then bring towel sides down around ball. Secure with rubber band and adjust gathers evenly. Conceal rubber band with ribbon tied in a bow.

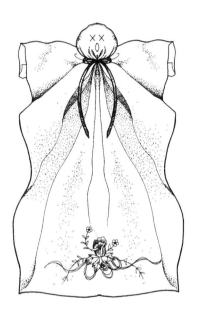

4 With one hand, squeeze together towel's side and doll's "shoulder." With your other hand, pull tightly on doll's "hand," as you loop it over your index finger. This will make the "arm" narrow enough to bring the "hand" through the loop, forming an overhand knot. Repeat for other side.

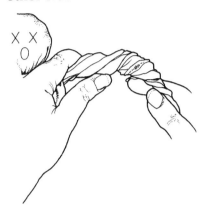

5 Adorn doll's head with purchased doll hair and/or hat, or make a bonnet from a 4"-diameter doily, shaped with two small darts stitched in back, and with ribbon ties added at each side.

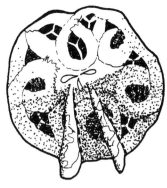

two small stitched darts

When deciding embellishments, evaluate the age appropriateness of the child for whom the doll is intended.

"My Aunt Mabel used to amuse me during church by taking a hankie from her purse and quickly tying it into a hankie doll similar to this Tea Towel Doll."
—Edna Powers

Gifts for All Occasions

Avoid any last minute rush for a gift by making ahead a few *Affordable Heirlooms*—suitable for nearly every gift-giving occasion. They're sure to be appreciated by any mother or daughter, teacher or hostess, friend or neighbor, graduate or grandma.

If you fidget in front of a television because your hands would rather be busy, bring along a needle, thread, and stack of hankies. Our pretty pockets, called Treasure Envelopes, are so simple that you could make several during your favorite show.

In a matter of minutes you can insert a small or leftover linen piece into a premade needlework card. Personalize your message for the occasion, and you have a handy, hand-made gift.

Treasure Envelopes

A single linen (such as a hankie, cocktail napkin, or doily) and length of ribbon can (with the help of a few folds and hand stitches) be transformed into a Treasure Envelope—a little linen package. Although Treasure Envelopes vary in shape, you'll discover that each one has a secret pocket.

Perhaps you'll tuck a bit of treasure inside, such as a small gift, love note, dried flowers, or wrapped candy. Add a ribbon hanger to any of the Treasure Envelopes to hang them on a wall, individually or grouped, empty or with a sprig of dried flowers slipped inside. Treasure Envelopes also make splendid Christmas ornaments. You may decide that your Treasure Envelope is delightful enough to use or to give as is.

For each of these projects, one or more applications of starch will be necessary to give the linen support. *Do not* press any of the folds, as rounded edges have more dimension than creases.

> "*J*oann Collins wanted to donate a generous stack of starched and ironed hankies to me because she didn't know what else to do with them. I convinced her to use some ideas in this book and thus pass on some of the hankies to her family."
> —Edna Powers

Square Fold

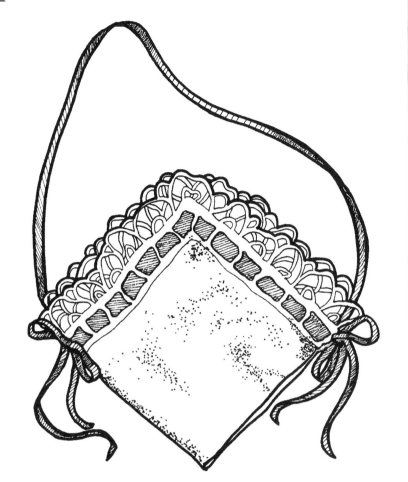

Procedure

1 Position linen diagonally wrong side up. Fold linen in half wrong sides together.

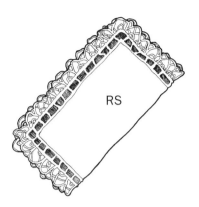

RS

2 Fold in half again so that all four corners are together at the top. Invisibly hand-stitch the double-folded edges together to create a pocket. The top corners may be paired and tacked together, if desired.

*"**W**hen my husband's grandmother died, I asked only for her button collection—stored in a large, round, metal container. Gary recalls spending hours as a child sifting and sorting through that box, just as I have done with my children, Genna and Garrison. Mamaw's buttons together with my mother's hankie were the inspiration for the dress on page 24."*
—Gaye Kriegel

Corner Fold ✄

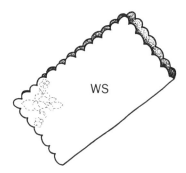

Procedure

1 Position linen diagonally right side up with the embellished corner located at the left.

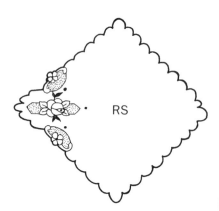

2 Fold the lower right half over the left upper half. (Linen's right sides are together and the embellishment on the under layer is temporarily covered.)

3 Fold in half again so that all four corners are together at the top. Invisibly hand-stitch the double-folded edges together to create a pocket. Fold down the uppermost single layer facing you to expose the embellished corner. The remaining three top corners may be tacked together, if desired.

Double-Point Fold

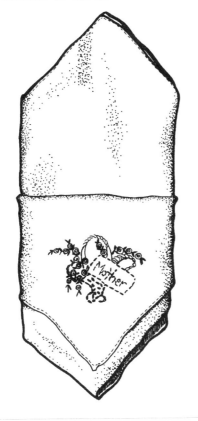

Procedure

Follow the directions for Corner Fold. Then fold the side corners underneath linen, overlap desired amount, and tack.

Border Fold

Procedure

1 Fold linen's edges toward each other, wrong sides together, so that the decorative lace borders overlap slightly. Secure with hand or machine stitches through all thicknesses.

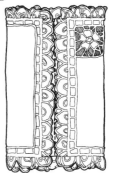

2 Fold perpendicular to borders, and sew the side folds together invisibly.

Heart-Shaped Holder

Procedure

1 Utilize openings of crocheted doilies to weave them together with ribbon, forming a holder. Depending on doily size, approximately one yard of 1/8" ribbon will connect doilies and serve as a hanger.

2 Pin two identically shaped doilies wrong sides together. Divide ribbon in half, and temporarily mark middle with a pin. Use a ribbon-weaving needle or a blunt-nose tapestry needle to weave each ribbon end along each side of doilies. Keep ribbon flat, and try to balance your ribbon stitches on each doily side.

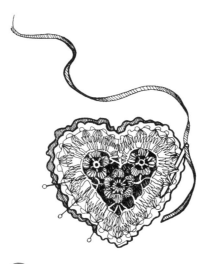

3 Leaving a loop at top for hanging, tie ribbon ends, into a bow at holder's bottom. (Doilies of any shape may be used in this manner.)

Greeting Cards

How wonderful to give a card so special that you know it will never be thrown away; so special, it's a gift in itself. Including a message in the card about the linen makes it all the more a keepsake. If it's too pretty to put away, try framing the card, or setting it on an easel.

Greeting cards are a great project for small embroidery pieces, especially those so fragile that they could never be washed repeatedly. Use the card's opening to focus on beautiful embellishment, even if the rest of the linen is damaged. Feature one special piece of embroidery, or combine several in a patchwork.

Select a card color and opening shape to complement the linen(s). Card may be accented with tiny buttons, bows, or rub-on lettering; or surround the card's opening with a drawn design, machine stitching, or lace trim.

Supplies

- triple-fold needlework card or heavyweight paper to make your own
- paper and pencil
- one or more small pieces of lightweight embellished linens
- glue stick
- underlining fabric for transparent linens
- small pieces of fleece for padded variations
- fabric glue, such as Unique Stitch, for candy cane or patchwork variations
- paper-backed fusible web and 1/16"-wide ribbon for patchwork variation

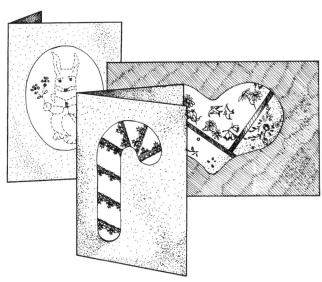

Needlework Cards

Triple-fold needlework cards have an opening through which linen is seen, a flap to conceal linen's underside, and a third section for card's message and back. (See Resources, page 115.) Depending on card's opening, it can be used vertically or horizontally.

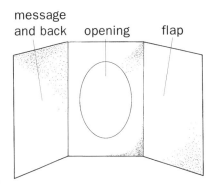

message and back   opening   flap

To make your own card, fold a piece of heavyweight paper into thirds. Trim flap edge slightly so that it does not pucker inside card. Draw or trace a design onto underside of center section, open card, and carefully cut out design using small, sharp scissors.

Procedure

1 The simplest card uses one linen, without padding. Unfold card and move its opening over linen, to select embellishment. Cut off excess linen, with plenty of margin around card's opening. Where possible, cut off bumpy linen hems, to keep card flatter.

2 Rub glue stick around wrong side of card's opening. (A piece of paper underneath opening will protect work surface.) Looking through right side of card opening, position it over right side of linen; then press card onto linen to secure. If linen is sheer, glue an underlining layer behind linen. A good underlining choice is a leftover solid section of the linen.

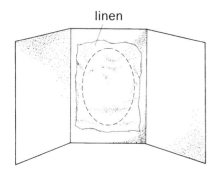

linen

3 Rub glue stick on back side of flap, especially around perimeter. (Again, paper will protect work surface.) Fold flap over linen, weigh down with books, and let dry thoroughly.

Padded Variation

Padding behind the linen adds significantly to the card's appeal. Padding can be added to the other variations as well.

Procedure

1 Before attaching linen, trace card's opening onto paper. Cut out paper and use as pattern to cut two to three layers of fleece. After linen and underlining are glued in place, apply glue stick on underlining, right around card opening, as well as to back side of flap. Position fleece on underlining, behind opening.

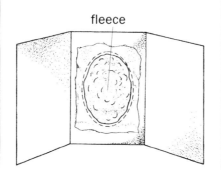

fleece

2 Fold flap over linen, finger-press tightly around card opening, weigh down with books, and let dry thoroughly.

3 To pad only part of the design, such as a bunny's tail or flower center, sew linen and underlining together almost all the way around selected area, push in a bit of fleece, and then finish sewing.

4 Follow general directions to complete card.

Candy Cane Variation

A white hankie with narrow red lace edging can be used to simulate a candy cane. Try it in a Christmas green-colored card.

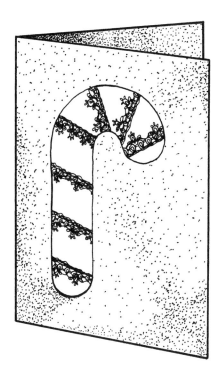

Procedure

1 Cut a 1"-wide strip (excluding lace) from the hankie's edge. (Rotary cutter and clear graph ruler are accurate tools for this step.) Cut the strip into seven 1-1/2"-long pieces.

2 Follow directions for making your own card, using pattern at right for the candy cane design. Trace the cut-out opening onto a paper. Cut a rectangle of underlining from remaining hankie, and lay it over paper. You need to see pattern's outline through underlining. Starting at candy cane's lower end, lay each cut linen section on underlining, overlapping cut edges with lace edges. Be sure that short ends of pieces extend past candy cane outline.

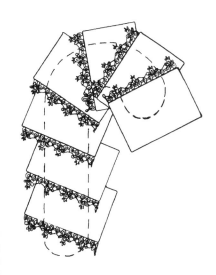

3 Try not to disturb your placement as you carefully lift one section at a time, apply a narrow line of fabric glue underneath hankie hem, and press onto lower layer.

4 Follow general directions to complete card.

See pattern below.

Candy Cane Pattern

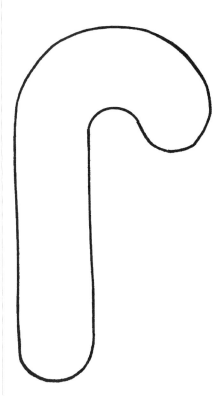

Patchwork Variation

Even smaller embellished pieces may be shown to full advantage in a patchwork. For a cohesive design, choose three or more linens that share a common element, such as color, style, or subject.

Procedure

1 Trace card opening onto paper. Cut embellished areas from linens with generous amounts of margin. Adhere paper-backed fusible web to undersides of cut pieces. Fit pieces together like a puzzle, by moving them around over paper drawing, overlapping in different combinations. Try to have embellished designs complement and fill card opening. Trim pieces where they overlap, and cut off excess margins. Butt pieces together on backing fabric and fuse.

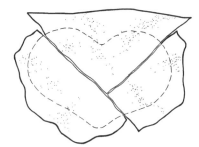

2 Cut lengths of 1/16"-wide ribbon to glue over butted edges, planning ahead so that, within the design, a cut ribbon end is covered by another ribbon.

3 Follow general directions to complete card.

*"**H**ome has always been a haven from the outside world—a place to shelter ourselves and our loved ones from the hurried pace and demands that exist beyond the threshold. Decorating with linens, especially old linens, provides comfort, as well as a comforting reminder of a simpler time."*
—Gaye Kriegel

Part IV

Home Decorating

Home has always been a haven from the outside world. With a little effort it can be both functional and beautiful. The textiles you choose to cover a bed or window play an integral part in expressing the feeling of your home. Every old linen has a story. Whether or not we know that story, the illusion is that someone spent hours stitching by hand, perhaps by candlelight, to embellish a simple cloth. Decorating with linens, especially old linens, provides comfort, as well as a reminder of a simpler time.

For the Kitchen

Colorful roosters embroidered on a set of linen placemats and napkins were the inspiration for these kitchen accessories. Although your linens will be different from our samples, the directions are adaptable to your linen choice and will provide your kitchen with a coordinated look.

Three placemats and three napkins provided enough fabric and embroidery for a potholder, oven mitt, towel band, toaster cover, and apron. Additional yardage was used for the apron and as lining for the oven mitt and toaster cover. A metallic ironing board cover was cut up for the undersides and padding of the potholder and oven mitt. (Metallic ironing board fabric is available through Nancy's Notions; see Resources, page 115.) A bathroom hand towel was attached to the decorative band.

A commercial pattern is *not* necessary for these projects—just use the following directions and patterns provided. You'll soon have enough confidence to try other accessories on your own, such as a teapot cozy, double oven mitt, and additional appliance covers.

Potholder

Supplies

- placemat or other suitable linen, prewashed
- 9" square each of metallic ironing board fabric and pad
- approximately 1 yard extra-wide double-fold bias tape
- pattern paper, pencil, ruler
- seam sealant, such as Fray Check, optional
- fabric glue, such as Unique Stitch, optional

Pattern

Draw an 8" square on a piece of paper. Use a form such as a drinking glass for a template to round each of the corners.

Preparation

Use pattern to cut your linen, centering the design, if possible. In our project, the design was so close to the placemat corner that not enough fabric surrounded the design to center it on potholder. But because the design was compact and tightly embroidered, it could be repositioned using the following technique.

1 Saturate perimeter of embroidered design on the top side with seam sealant, and let dry completely. Repeat on underside perimeter of design. Seam sealants usually dry clear but test on a scrap first.

2 Carefully cut around design, without cutting any embroidery threads. The 4" Gingher trimming scissors work well for this step.

3 Coat back of embroidered section with a fabric glue, and adhere to potholder fabric. Use a flat toothpick to remove any excess glue from around embroidery edges. Weigh down with books, and let dry thoroughly.

Procedure

1 The ironing board cover fabric has layers of silver metallic fabric and foam padding. Cut fabric and pad pieces about 1/2" larger all around than your pattern. Center and pin the decorative fabric, right side up, over pad, with metallic fabric on the bottom layer. Zigzag around decorative fabric edge, and then trim around outside of zigzag stitching. This method is easier than trying to keep the raw edges of three identically-sized pieces aligned while sewing.

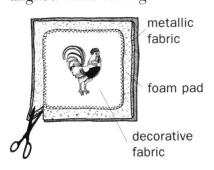

metallic fabric

foam pad

decorative fabric

2 Bind potholder edges with double-fold bias tape, beginning in the upper right corner. Stop stitching about 1" before you're completely around. Add about five more inches of binding; then cut.

3 To form a hanging loop, tuck binding's loose end under binding's front edge. Be sure to cover where your binding began, and then complete stitching.

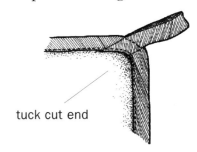

tuck cut end

*"**A**s I debated over whether to buy this set of Guatemalan embroidered linens, another shopper hovered nearby ready to grab them if I dared to lay them down."*
—Gaye Kriegel

*"**G**iven a hand-crocheted doily by a friend in France, I wanted to thank her in an appropriate way with a hand-made item that was easy to mail. Using her doily as a silhouette to block the sun from blueprint sensitive fabric, I then fashioned a potholder that bore the image of my friend's doily. The result was a hand-crafted, personal gift, lightweight for mailing."*
—Doris Hoover, author, **Too Hot To Handle, Potholders and How To Make Them**

Oven Mitt

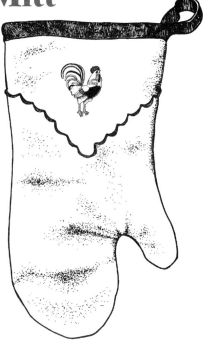

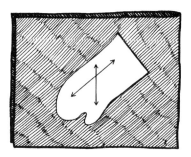

thickness of lining fabric, preferably on bias grain.

Supplies

- 15" napkin or other suitable linen, prewashed
- 10" x 15" rectangle each, metallic ironing board cover fabric and pad
- 21" of extra-wide double-fold bias tape
- 1/2 yard cotton or poly/cotton blend fabric for lining
- fusible web such as Stitch Witchery, optional

Pattern

Enlarge the pattern on page 77 by 200%, using a photocopy machine or by drawing on a 1/2" grid. The mitt's open end should measure about 7-3/4".

Preparation

1 Cut pattern shape from the linen. (For a pair of mitts, place two linens right sides together, and cut simultaneously.) The mitt opening is decorated with linen's embellished corner. Measure an equal amount down each side from embellished corner, and cut off diagonally.

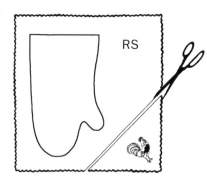

2 Turn pattern over, and cut layers of ironing board fabric and pad about 1/2" larger all around than pattern. Use pattern to cut double

Procedure

1 Lay embellished corner over mitt fabric, both right sides up, centering corner's tip in middle of mitt. Decide how far down on mitt the corner tip will extend. (Sample is 6-1/2".) Either topstitch corner to mitt or slip two strips of fusible web under corner, and fuse according to product directions. Trim excess corner fabric even with mitt shape.

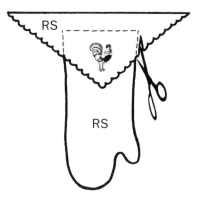

2 Pin mitt fabric to metallic ironing board fabric, right sides together, with pad as bottom layer. Sew a 1/4"-wide seam, using edge of presser foot on linen edge as a guide and leaving top edge

open. This method is easier than trying to keep the raw edges of three identically-sized pieces aligned while sewing. Curves are easier to sew accurately and are smoother after turning if you sew with about 16 stitches per inch.

stitching about 1" before you're completely around. Measure about five more inches of binding, and cut. To form a hanging loop, tuck binding's loose end under binding's front edge. Be sure to cover where your binding began, and then complete stitching.

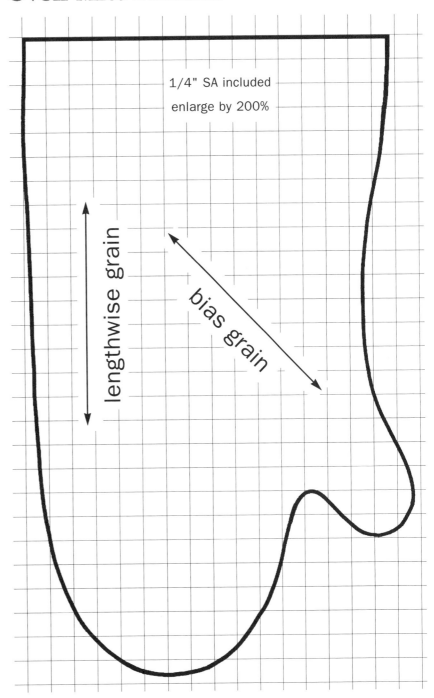

tuck cut end

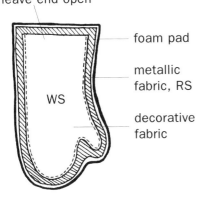

leave end open

foam pad

metallic fabric, RS

WS

decorative fabric

3 Trim seam allowances even all around close to stitching, using pinking shears. (If you don't have pinking shears, notch curves with scissors.) Turn right side out and press.

4 Sew lining pieces, right sides together, in a 3/8"-wide seam, so lining will be slightly smaller than mitt. Slip lining into mitt, wrong sides together. Align top edges, and zigzag around top through all thicknesses.

5 Bind top edge with double-fold bias tape, beginning at thumb side. Stop

Oven Mitt Pattern

1/4" SA included

enlarge by 200%

lengthwise grain

bias grain

Towel Band

|← 5" →|

2 Sandwich cut end of towel between the wrong sides of both napkin corners. Topstitch band layers to towel, and then continue stitching along remaining band edges.

Supplies

- bathroom hand towel, about 16" x 29", pre-washed
- napkin (minimum 12") or other suitable linen, prewashed
- 1 yard of extra-wide double-fold bias tape
- pattern paper, pencil

Preparation

Cut towel in half cross-wise. Use the other half for another purpose or another towel band. Cut one embellished corner and one plain corner from the linen, using pattern on page 79. Position pattern corner along linen's finished edges.

Procedure

1 Fold and pin towel, overlapping the folds in back, if necessary, so that width of top cut edge

3 Bind top edge of band. Then cut two 15" pieces of binding for the band sides and ties. Fold under binding's lower cut ends, and bind sides of band, continuing to sew binding edges together above band. Tie an overhand knot in each tie end, to prevent raveling.

Towel Band Pattern

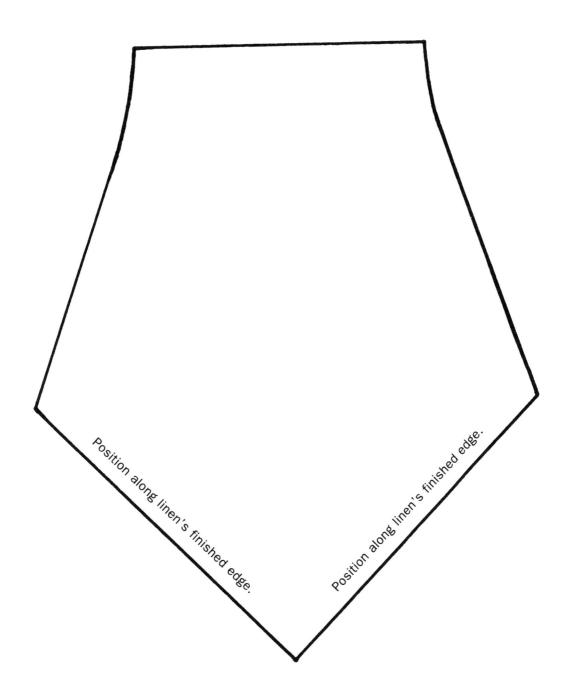

Position along linen's finished edge.

Position along linen's finished edge.

Toaster Cover

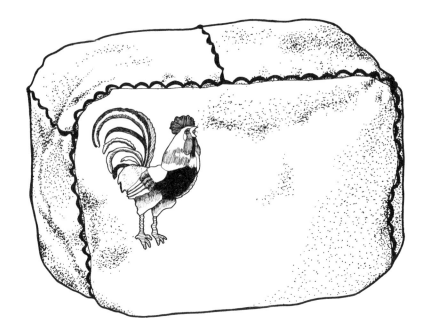

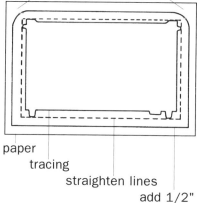

off the upper two corners slightly. This is the pattern for the front and back sections.

round top corners

paper

tracing

straighten lines

add 1/2"

Supplies

- 2 placemats or other suitable linens, prewashed
- 4 linen pieces leftover from previously sewn kitchen accessories
- 1/2 yard cotton or poly/cotton lining fabric
- 1/2 yard 1/4"-thick fleece
- pattern paper (graph paper suggested), pencil, ruler
- fabric glue, such as Unique Stitch, optional

Note: If preferred, metallic ironing board fabric and pad or three pre-quilted fabric placemats can substitute for lining fabric and fleece.

Option: A piping may be added in the cover's seams, although more time and skill is required. (The trimmed-off scalloped edges from placemats were used as a piping in sample project's front seam only.)

Pattern

1 Given the variety of toaster sizes, it's virtually impossible that a commercial pattern will fit your toaster. Save money by making your own pattern, and then use this technique to make custom-sized covers for other kitchen appliances.

2 Lay the (clean) toaster horizontally on a piece of paper. Trace around toaster's perimeter, including projections, such as handles and legs. Use graph paper lines or a ruler to draw straight lines outside any projections. Then increase your rectangle by 1/2" all around, for ease and seam allowances. Round

3 Set toaster upright. For the top/sides section, measure depth of toaster, adding 1" for two seam allowances and ease. Then measure from the table, up one side of toaster, across its top, and down other side to table. Add 3" to this measurement, and plan on trimming excess later. Either record these measurements or make a paper pattern.

Preparation

1 Cut a front and a back from the linens. Remember the rounded corners of pattern are at top of cover.

2 To get a fabric strip long enough for top/sides section, use four pieces of linens left over from previously sewn kitchen accessories. Lap finished edge of one piece over cut edge of another piece, and secure with topstitching or fabric

Affordable Heirlooms

glue. Trim this strip of joined pieces according to your top/sides measurements or pattern, noting that the midpoint of this section is where the second and third pieces are joined.

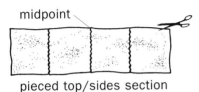

midpoint

pieced top/sides section

3 Cut front, back, and top/sides pieces from both lining and fleece. If replacing lining and fleece layers with prequilted fabric placemats, cut them to size, seaming two leftover pieces for top/sides section.

Procedure

1 Pin one edge of top/sides piece to front, right sides together, starting at midpoint of top, and then proceeding down each side. Ease top/sides piece to fit

by making tiny clips in its seam allowance for 1" on either side of each top corner. Sew with a 1/4"-wide seam allowance.

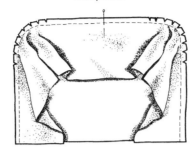

midpoint

2 Repeat steps to join opposite edge of top/sides piece to back piece. Trim any excess top/sides section even with lower edges of front and back pieces.

3 To pad lining pieces, back each one with corresponding fleece piece, and sew together in a grid or diamond pattern. Repeat assembly procedure to sew padded lining pieces to each other.

4 Fit lining and cover pieces over toaster to determine exact width of lower seam allowance. Mark with a pin.

5 Slip lining over cover, right sides together, matching seams, pinning seam allowances toward front and back, and then sew bottom seam.

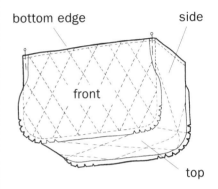

bottom edge   side

front

top

6 Tuck lining inside the outer cover, wrong sides together, and press the bottom edge.

*"**T**he textiles you choose for your home play an integral part in the feeling your home expresses, even as they perform their functional duty of covering a bed or window or table."*
—Gaye Kriegel

Apron

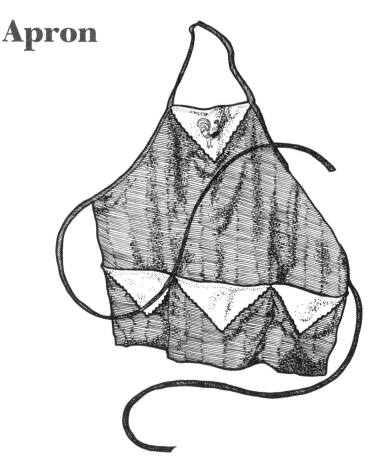

Supplies

- 2 napkins or other suitable linens, prewashed
- 1 yard of broadcloth (looks the same on both sides), prewashed
- 3-3/4 yards extra-wide double-fold bias tape
- pattern paper, pencil, ruler
- washable marking pen or chalk
- fusible laminate, such as HeatnBond or Kittrich, optional
- fusible web such as Stitch Witchery, optional

Pattern

1 Measure and label a rectangle of paper 18" x 36", as shown. For pocket section, draw a line 9" from bottom.

2 Along one side mark a point at 26". At top, mark 6" from center fold. Connect these two points in a curve.

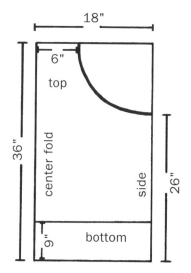

Preparation

1 Fold fabric in half lengthwise. Align pattern center fold with fabric fold, cut around pattern. For pocket, fold up 9" from bottom, press. (If both sides of your fabric are not identical, cut off the 9" pocket section, and seam its right side to apron wrong side, along apron lower edge. Then press pocket section to apron right side concealing seam.)

2 Use embellished linen corners for apron top and middle pocket. Use plain corners for the other two pockets. Or use a plain corner leftover from another project for middle pocket. On linen, measure and mark 8" down each side of selected corners. Draw a line between the marks and cut with scissors, or connect marks with ruler and use rotary cutter.

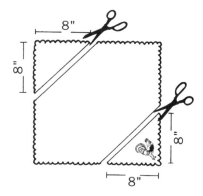

Procedure

1 Fuse optional laminate following product directions, but be aware that laminating makes fabric crisp.

2 To finish apron's top edge, place right side of embellished linen corner against wrong side of apron. Sew a 1/4"-wide seam allowance.

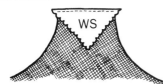

3 Understitch seam allowance to apron, then press linen corner to apron's front side. Either topstitch corner's finished edges to apron, or fuse with strips of fusible web.

4 Open out pocket section with the back-side up. Align cut edges of the three remaining linen corners along pocket edge. The right side of linen is against back side of pocket edge; the tip of middle corner matches center of apron; and the edges overlap each other by 1/2". Linens will probably *not* extend entire length of pocket edge. Sew a 1/4"-wide seam allowance.

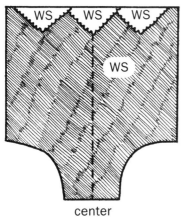

center

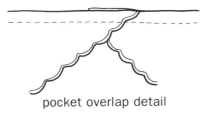

pocket overlap detail

5 Understitch seam allowance to pocket section, then press linens to front side. The overlapped corners of linens will cover the seam allowance. Secure linens' finished edges to pocket section by topstitching or by fusing with strips of fusible web.

6 Reposition pocket section over apron front. Topstitch from the overlapped corners down to bottom fold line through all thicknesses to divide into three pockets. Trim excess fabric from apron sides 1/2" beyond the outside napkin corners. Hem apron sides: serge off 1/4", press under 1/4" and stitch; or press under 1/4" twice and stitch.

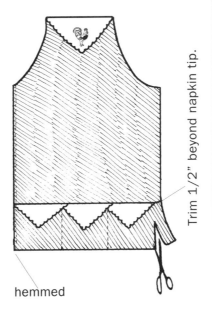

hemmed

Trim 1/2" beyond napkin tip.

7 Divide the double-fold bias tape in half, and mark center point temporarily with a pin. Measure 12" from this pin; then insert and pin top corner of apron there. Repeat for other side.

Try on apron, and adjust neck strap length if necessary. Tuck curved apron edges into binding and pin.

Zigzag or topstitch from one binding tip continuously to the other tip, sewing together the binding edges and securing the curved apron edges as you come to them.

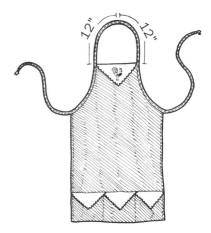

12"   12"

8 Tie binding ends in overhand knots, to prevent raveling.

For the Bathroom

It may be called the "necessary room," but it can also be beautiful with the addition of these accessories. Towels, tissue boxes, toilet paper, and even the sink counter can be enhanced with linens. Sew a single item or a complete ensemble—for your own bathroom or for a welcomed gift.

Since these items will require frequent washings, select either new linens or old linens that are still in good condition.

Tissue Box Cover

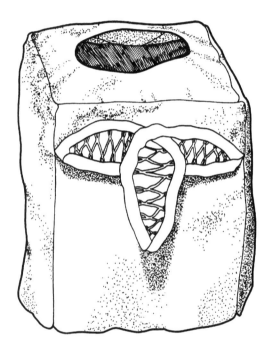

Supplies

- cube-style box of tissue
- paper, pencil, ruler
- linen napkin, approximately 14" square, with one embellished corner
- crisp fusible interfacing, same size as napkin

Note: These directions may be adapted for a rectangular tissue box, but you will need two napkins.

Pattern

Note: In the upcoming directions 3/8" additions are added to traced lines, which allows for a 1/4" seam allowance plus ease to slip the cover over the box. When sewing around the top's opening, the extra amount will cover the box's top when it's inside.

1 Since box sizes vary by brand, it's best to measure your box for a custom fit. Trace a box side, draw an arrow on the paper to indicate vertical direction, and add 3/8" to pattern top and sides. Using the napkin's hem eliminates the need for a hem allowance.

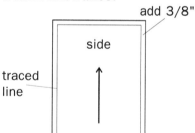

2 Trace box's top, and add 3/8" to each edge. Draw the opening shape in the pattern's center by tracing the perforated cardboard piece that is removed to open the box. Mark a cutting line 3/8" *inside* this oval.

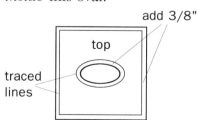

Affordable Heirlooms

Procedure

1 Pin side pattern piece under napkin's embellished corner, to determine placement. Cut corner from napkin; then trim even with pattern sides. Cut one top pattern piece (including the oval opening) for lining.

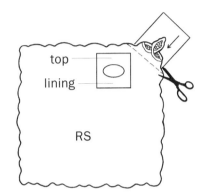

2 Fuse interfacing, according to product directions, to wrong side of remaining napkin piece. Cut four sides, aligning pattern's bottom edge with napkin's finished edge. Cut top pattern (including the oval opening) once more.

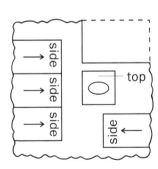

3 Pin embellished corner to one side piece, both right sides up.

4 Aligning finished hem edges, sew the four sides, right sides together, using a 1/4"-wide seam allowance.

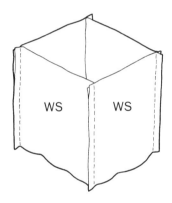

5 Check fit by slipping this section over box. Sew each seam a bit deeper, if necessary, but there's no need to rip out original seams.

6 Place the two top pieces right sides together, and sew around opening using a 1/4"-wide seam allowance. Clip into seam allowance close to stitching.

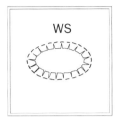

7 Turn top section right side out and press flat. Pin top section to side section, right sides together, matching each top corner to one side seam. Sew around top, using a 1/4"-wide seam allowance, pivoting at each corner.

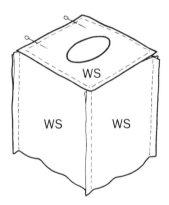

8 Turn cover right side out, press, and slip over box.

Toilet Paper Sling

Supplies

- embellished tea towel, at least 12" x 20"
- cardboard tube, removed from dry cleaner pants hanger
- 18" to 27" narrow decorative cord

Procedure

1 Fold towel lengthwise, right sides together centering motif on fold. Measure and pin 5-1/2" from fold. Sew along this pin line, trim

excess seam allowance, and press seam open.

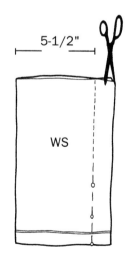

2 Turn towel right side out, then rotate it to position seam allowance at center back.

3 Slide towel's embellished end over the opposite towel end, forming a loop. Topstitch to join ends.

Insert inside embellished end.

4 Cut cardboard tube to width of sling. Drop one cord end through cardboard tube, and position tube inside sling. Tie cord ends together, adjusting length, as desired; then pull cord until knot is concealed inside tube. Place toilet paper roll inside sling, and hang cord on hook. Optional decorative bow could be used to hide hook.

Counter Skirt

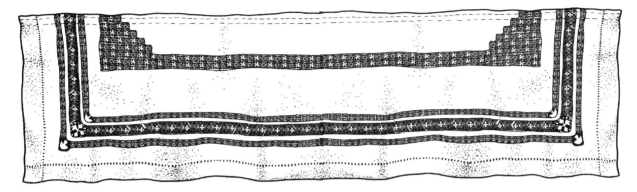

Select a long dresser scarf or a section of tablecloth that is at least as long as the sink counter.

Procedure

1 A finished long edge will be used for the hem. Press under and sew the opposite long edge, determining the finished skirt height, which can be as short as about 10" or can extend to the floor.

2 Decide whether skirt will fit flush with counter or incorporate any extra length by gathering or pleating. Hem side edges, if they are not already finished.

3 After all hemming is complete, and any gathers or pleats are secured, sew the soft side of hook-and-loop tape to wrong side of upper skirt edge. Glue or staple the opposite tape to sink counter. Press tapes together to hang skirt yet allow easy removal for washing.

4 Further embellish with bows, if desired. A similar procedure could be used for a dressing table skirt.

Embellished Towels

Embellishment choices such as doilies, embroidered bands, or recycled pillow-case edgings should be selected in proportion to towel size. Color combinations can match or contrast, as desired.

Procedure

Prewash and dry all items to control shrinkage. Zigzag embellishment's finished edge to towel, using thread to match embellishment. Illustrated here are three ideas.

For the Bed or Sofa

Pillows can provide comfort, set a style, or spark a conversation. Whether they are intended for service or beauty, pillows made from embellished linens are sure to capture attention.

For such small projects, pillows pack a big decorating punch, easily changed with the seasons or your style. Pillows are also the perfect project for playing with creative ideas and techniques. With minimal effort and expense, you can impact a room's mood—a little or a lot. Husbands who might balk at frilly curtains may not be at all bothered by an embroidered pillow or two. (Three?)

Some of the following projects could utilize plain pillows that you purchase or already have; then you can proceed directly to the embellishment. Some ideas, techniques, shapes, and edgings may be interchanged. Your particular linens may inspire new designs.

Since the basics of assembling pillows is sufficiently covered by many other sources, the following instructions focus specifically on designing pillows embellished with linens. Here are four questions to ask yourself as you design your pillow.

1 *Do I plan to lie on, lean against, or just look at this pillow?* Embellishments of buttons, silk flowers, pouf bows, or other projections should be limited to the just-look-at pillow styles. Otherwise, the embellishment, your back, or both, will suffer.

2 *Do I need an edge design for this pillow?* Edgings can frame the pillow (focusing attention on the linen), increase the pillow's size, and be beautiful as well. Options include one or more corded pipings, sewn ruffles, lace trims, or corded piping plus a ruffle, lace plus a ruffle, or a shirred corded piping.

3 *Do I plan to wash this pillow?* If so, fabrics, linens, and non-removable embellishments must all be washable. Covers should be removed for washing, since few pillow forms or fillings maintain their shape.

Removable covers open and close using the same methods as clothing: zippers, buttons, snaps, ties, elastic, hook-and-loop tape, or simply two sections in the back that overlap each other.

Unlike clothing, pillow covers can be sewn closed if you don't anticipate frequent washings, or if you don't mind re-sewing the opening after washing. Our samples were sewn closed, but you may substitute another closure method.

4 *What should I use to fill the pillow?* Linen sizes rarely coincide with standard-size pillow forms. But don't dismay; custom-sized forms are easy to make.

To avoid an unattractive lumpy surface, sew fleece layers under the pillow top and back, before stuffing the pillow. Not only is this method less expensive than ready-made pillow forms, you are free to design pillows of any shape, size, or firmness.

Transparent or fragile linens benefit from an underlining of batiste, in addition to the fleece. Good quality fiberfill, such as Mountain Mist or Fairfield, helps produce a smoother pillow, as well.

Although you may generally prefer the softness of fiberfill to the sturdiness of foam forms, they do assure a perfect shape for roll-style pillows. Specialty foam shops have roll forms in a variety of diameters, moderately priced, and easily cut to needed length with a serrated kitchen knife.

Single Hankie Pillows

Please read the general information at the beginning of this chapter. If you do not have pillow-making experience, supplement the following specific directions from another source.

One-Corner Hankie Pillow

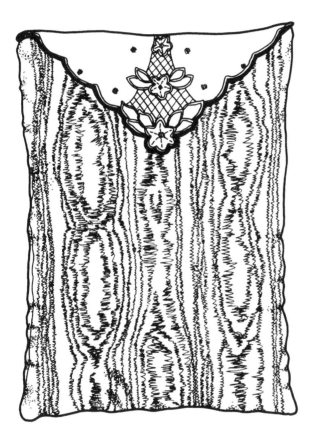

The following illustrations show how a pillow shape can vary from square to rectangular, and use more or less of the same embellished hankie corner, depending where it's cut.

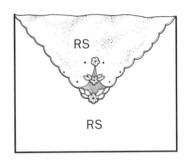

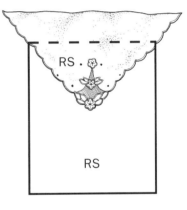

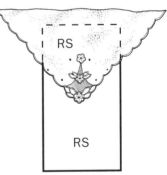

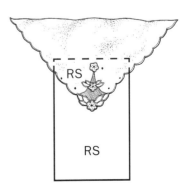

Procedure

1 When you've decided on complementary shapes, cut fabric for pillow top, including seam allowances. Pin hankie to fabric, both right sides up; then trim hankie edges even with fabric.

2 Topstitching hankie's finished edge to fabric is optional.

3 Assemble pillow, stuff, and close.

Wrapped Hankie Pillow

Procedure

1 Measure hankie diagonally, and make a pillow whose finished sides are *half* that measurement, plus 1/2". For example, if hankie measures 16" diagonally, make an 8-1/2" square pillow.

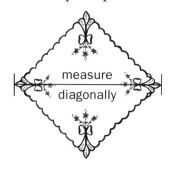

measure
diagonally

2 Set completed pillow on wrong side of hankie, aligning hankie corners with pillow sides.

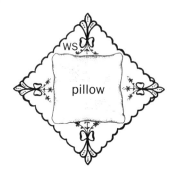

ws
pillow

3 Bring hankie corners around pillow sides to meet at pillow center. Tack hankie corners to pillow top, adding a button or bow if appropriate.

Scrunched Hankie Pillow

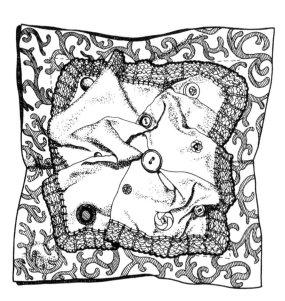

Procedure

1 Make (or use ready-made) pillow approximately 2" smaller than hankie. Pin hankie corners somewhat near pillow corners.

2 Randomly fold over excess hankie fullness, and pin to pillow. Use folds to hide any tears or stains.

3 Hand-sew matching or assorted buttons to secure hankie folds to pillow.

Hankie Border Pillow

Procedure

1 Cut lace-edged hankie in half. Position pieces so that lace edges are facing each other and separated as much as desired. Cut fabric for pillow top, adding seam allowances beyond upper and lower lace edges. Baste hankie's cut edges to pillow top's sides.

2 To prevent hankie corners from catching in top and bottom seam allowances, temporarily fold corners toward pillow center, and pin.

3 Cut fabric for pillow back and, if desired, an edge treatment.

4 Assemble pillow, but before turning right side out, reach inside and carefully remove pins holding hankie corners.

5 After pillow is turned, stuffed, and closed, tack hankie corners to pillow top.

"This linen was far too white in comparison to the muted colors of the printed panné velvet. The solution to the problem was simply dunking the linen in tea."
—*Gaye Kriegel*

"To make a linen look especially old and streaked, tea-dye it and then press it while it's still wet."
—*Debra Justice, owner of Labours of Love*

Layered Linen Pillows

Please read the general information at the beginning of this chapter. If you do not have pillow-making experience, supplement the following specific directions from another source.

Collage Pillow

Procedure

1 Collect an assortment of linens or pieces salvaged from otherwise unusable linens. They may have something in common, such as color or technique, or they may be widely divergent.

2 Decide whether the fabric will be prominent, with a contrasting color to showcase cut work or drawn work techniques, or merely serve as an underlining, concealed entirely by the linens. Cut fabric to size of pillow top plus seam allowances.

3 Begin layering linen pieces onto pillow top, all right sides up. Use finished edges to hide cut edges, or fold cut edges under. Cut edges may also be covered with ribbon or other trim. Conceal or cut away any damaged linen areas.

4 Experiment with covering all fabric or letting some show, trimming underneath linen layers or letting them stay. Keep shuffling your pieces until you like the arrangement; then pin together and topstitch to fabric along linen's finished edges. Cut excess linen pieces even with pillow top perimeter.

5 Cut fabric for back and, if desired, for an edge treatment. Assemble pillow, stuff, and close. Accent with buttons or bows, if appropriate.

"From the age of two, I remember looking forward to visiting our family friend Robbie to find the latest appliquéd, embroidered, or quilted addition. The most interesting area was a couch loaded with handmade pillows. My brother and I would kneel on the floor and gaze from one pillow to the next trying to find our favorite. Robbie died in a fire when she was 99 but I feel that she is with me every day—her salvageable heirlooms are all over my home."
—Jan Saunders, co-author, Sew & Serge Series

Tatted Edges Pillow

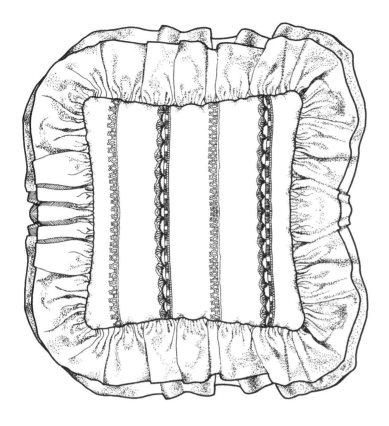

Procedure

1 Cut two lace-edged hankies in half. Alternating from each hankie, layer and pin pieces 2" apart, excluding lace.

2 Run a thin line of fabric glue, such as Unique Stitch, along the hemmed hankie edge where tatting is attached. Press onto underneath hankie layer. After glue is dry, cut off under-neath hankie layers close to glued edges.

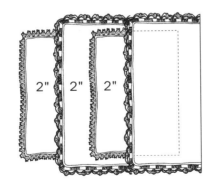

3 Trim excess from the far right hankie half, leaving a 2"-wide strip. Take that cut-off hankie piece and glue it under the first row of tatting, making a total of five sections. Trim far left sec-tion, if necessary, for a fin-ished width of 2".

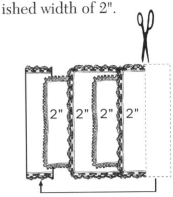

Trim off and relocate.

4 Trim tatting from han-kies' top and bottom edges, saving the pieces for another project, of course.

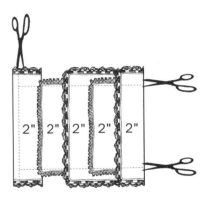

5 Underline pillow with batiste and fleece. If desired, edge with one or more bias-cut ruffles. Assemble pillow with a 1/4"-wide seam allowance, stuff, and sew opening closed.

Victorian Heart Pillow

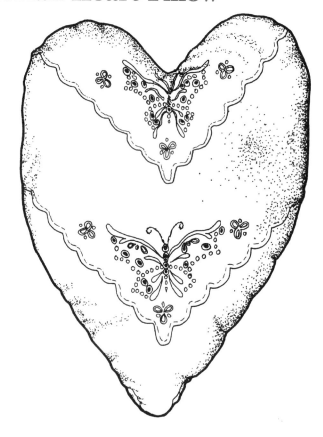

Procedure

1 Select two napkins, each at least 12" square, with one embellished corner. Enlarge pattern on page 95.

2 For pillow back, cut pattern shape from first napkin, reserving 4" at bottom corner for pillow front's top layer.

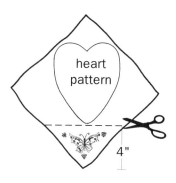

3 Cut second napkin in half diagonally. Use embellished half for front's middle layer, and other half (turned upside down), for front's bottom layer.

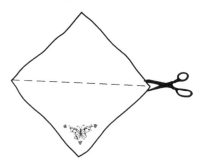

4 Assemble the three front layers, all with right sides up, over pattern, adjusting to fit; then pin layers together and remove pattern. Edgestitch middle and bottom layers together along napkin's decorative edge, using a narrow zigzag. Trim excess bottom napkin close to stitching. Then edgestitch top layer to middle layer and trim excess middle layer. After pressing layers, replace pattern and cut into heart shape.

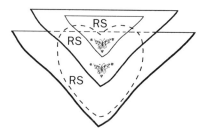

5 Underline pillow front and back with batiste, if needed, and then with fleece. Sew pillow front and back, right sides together, using a 1/4"-wide seam allowance and leaving an opening to stuff. Notch curved seam allowances. Turn right side out, stuff, and sew opening closed.

See pattern next page.

Victorian Heart Pattern

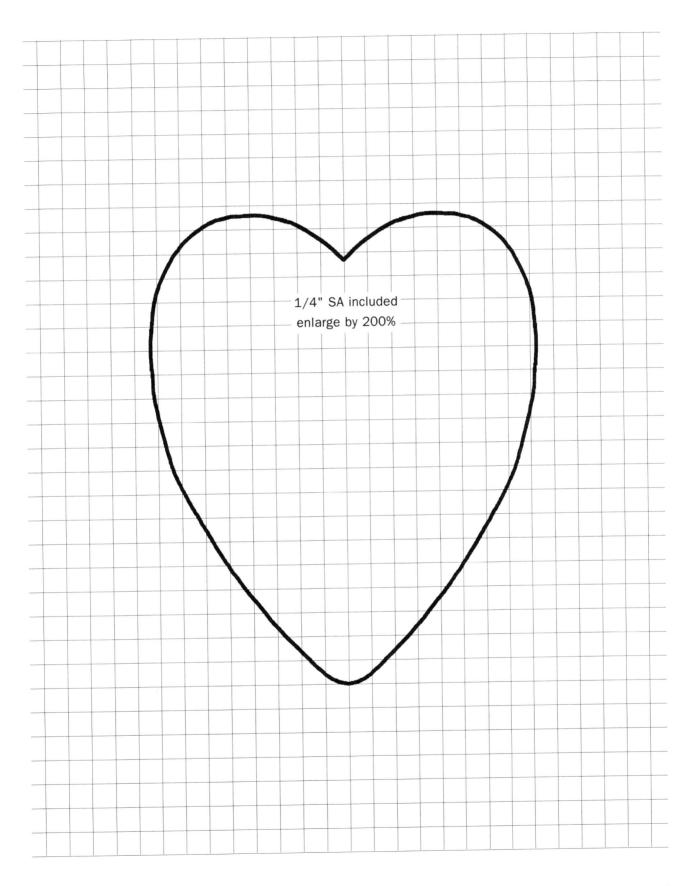

1/4" SA included
enlarge by 200%

Four-Layer Pillow

Procedure

1 Select two same-size hankies and one larger hankie. Pin the larger hankie, right side up, to an even larger piece of white felt, and sew together using narrow zigzag stitches at hankie's lace edging.

Carefully trim excess felt close to stitching.

2 Center one of the smaller hankies on top of first hankie, and topstitch at lace edging, through all thicknesses. Sew tucks through center of third hankie to reduce its size, and then join to pillow by sewing buttons at each hankie corner. Attach center of a crocheted doily to center of pillow top by sewing through doily and through a large button, then back down through doily and pillow top.

3 Lay felt side of completed pillow top onto a larger felt piece for pillow back. Narrowly zigzag around perimeter, on top of previous stitching, leaving an opening to stuff. Trim excess felt close to stitching, stuff pillow, and sew opening closed.

*"**N**ever pass up the chance to buy someone's button box at a garage sale, rummage sale, or thrift shop. This is where I've found many of my favorite treasures, and I always feel lucky to be the new owner. These button boxes usually are not just home to buttons. The last one I bought also contained bits of broken jewelry; a few real pearls; a 1917 penny; a thimble; marbles; and miscellaneous hooks, eyes, and snaps."*
—Marilyn Green, author, The Button Lover's Book

Assorted Linen Pillows

Please read the general information at the beginning of this chapter. If you do not have pillow-making experience, supplement the following specific directions from another source.

No-Sew Pillow

Procedure

1 Select two same-size hankies. Make (or use ready-made) pillow, approximately 2" smaller than hankies. Set pillow in between wrong sides of hankies.

2 Cinch hankies at pillow corners, and secure with small rubber bands. Conceal rubber bands with ribbon, cord, or something else decorative. Sample pillow has holly picks tucked under metallic stretch cord (intended for Christmas packages).

3 Replace corner treatments for variety, or remove them to wash hankies.

Envelope Pillow

Procedure

1 Select tea towel with one embellished end. Fold up opposite end and pin, wrong sides together, using just over two-thirds of towel length. Topstitch sides of pillow cover, sewing on top of towel's original side hems.

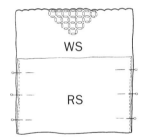

2 Make (or use ready-made) pillow insert to fit inside cover. Fold embellished towel end down, either leaving it free or securing it to lower layer. This technique could also be used to make a lingerie bag or clutch purse, if the linen were suitable.

Button Edge Pillow

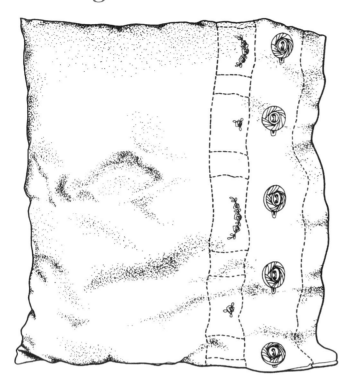

2 Turn towel right side out and press. Make (or use ready-made) pillow insert that will fit inside towel cover, up to but not past button area.

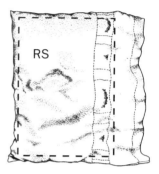

3 To actually button the cover around pillow insert, sew buttonholes in cover front, and sew buttons to inside edge of cover back. Or omit buttonholes, put insert inside cover, and sew buttons on pillow top, catching pillow back simultaneously.

Procedure

1 Fuse interfacing strips to wrong side of tea towel edges, where buttons and buttonholes are planned. Fold towel in half crosswise, right sides together. Seam towel sides, either by serging or by sewing and trimming close to stitching.

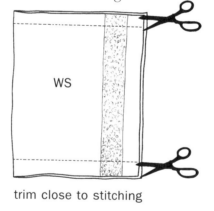

trim close to stitching

"My daughter, Kimberlee, rarely shared my enthusiasm for the old linens I brought home, until recently, when she gradually developed an appreciation for them. Now she's finding linens to decorate her apartment."
—Edna Powers

Affordable Heirlooms

Bordered Napkin Pillow

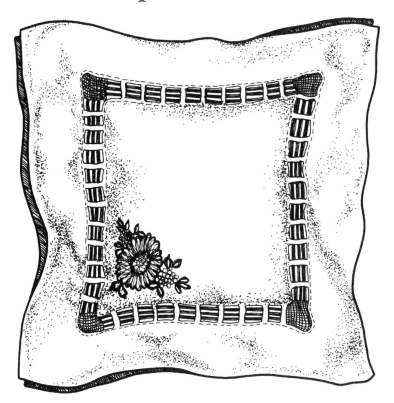

Procedure

1 Select two napkins that have woven borders around their perimeters. Pin them wrong sides together and sew along border, leaving an opening for stuffing.

2 Insert fiberfill; then sew opening closed. (A zipper foot is helpful for this step.)

3 Emphasize border, if desired. Our pillow has three 1/16"-wide ribbons woven through napkin's border to complement the embroidery colors.

"I remember trying to convince my mother that paper napkins were the 'in' thing to use at evening meals but she would calmly say, 'No, we'll use the linen, as usual.' I was responsible for ironing all those linen napkins."
—Barbara Bowers

Roll-Style Pillows

Please read the general information at the beginning of this chapter. If you do not have pillow-making experience, supplement the following specific directions from another source.

For roll-style pillows, fabric "width" covers around form's circumference, and fabric "length" covers form's length.

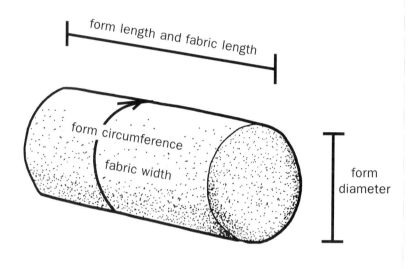

Pillowcase Pillow

Procedure

1 Carefully remove lace edging from pillowcase and temporarily set aside.

2 Cut off the end seam opposite the pillowcase opening. Cut pillowcase (on side seam if there is one) to open flat and use as the pillow fabric. Measure circumference of roll form and cut fabric 2" wider. Add together form length plus diameter plus two times finished size of end ruffle. Cut fabric that length.

3 Narrowly hem one long edge. To finish short ends, glue 1/8"-wide ribbon to right side of cut edges.

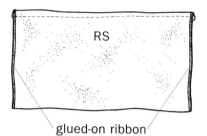

glued-on ribbon

4 Wrap fabric around form, lapping hemmed edge over cut edge, and hand-sew closed. Cinch fabric at form ends to create ruffles, secure with rubber bands, and conceal rubber bands with ribbon.

5 Drape, pin, and then hand-sew the previously removed lace edging along pillow top, easing in fullness around pillow ends.

6 To make removable poufs, hand-sew together several loops of 6"-wide tulle and 1/8"-wide ribbon. Dip bottom ends of silk rosebuds in glue, nestle them in between tulle loops, and let dry. Safety pin a pouf to each ruffle's ribbon-covered rubber band.

Tied Hankie Pillow

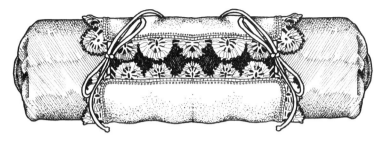

Procedure

1 Measure circumference of form, and cut fabric 2" wider. Add together roll form length plus diameter, subtract 1/2", and cut fabric that length. Narrowly hem one long edge, and sew gathering threads near cut edges of each short end.

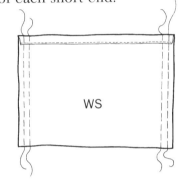

WS

2 Wrap fabric around form, lapping hemmed edge over cut edge, and hand-sew closed. Pull bobbin threads at ends to gather tightly, and then knot.

3 Make matching fabric-covered buttons, and glue over gathered ends.

4 Wrap hankie around pillow, and secure at sides by tying narrow fabric tubes, ribbon, or cord through openings in hankie's lace edging. If hankie pulls away from pillow at center, tack hankie to pillow cover.

Tea Towel Pillow

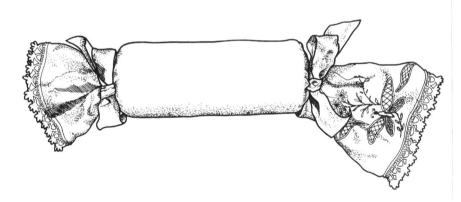

Procedure

1 Wrap a tea towel around roll form, and hand-sew lengthwise edges closed.

2 Create ruffles by grasping each towel end and securing with small rubber bands. Conceal rubber bands with decorative ribbon or cord.

"**M**y most vivid memory of my grandmother Emma is watching her crochet for hours never using a pattern. When I married, she gave me 32 pairs of trimmed pillowcases."
—Lenora Brancato

Lace-Band Ruffle Pillow

Procedure

1 Measure circumference of form and cut fabric 2" wider. Add together roll form length plus diameter plus four times finished size of end ruffle plus 2" for tucking in. Cut fabric that length.

2 Narrowly hem one long edge. Fold under each end the finished size of ruffle plus the 1" tuck-in, and sew together with gathering threads.

fold
doubled ruffle
1" tuck-in
1" tuck-in
doubled ruffle
fold

3 Wrap fabric around form, lapping hemmed edge over cut edge, and hand-sew closed. Pull bobbin threads to gather tightly and knot, creating ruffles.

4 To make "lace-edged rubber bands," cut two 3"-long pieces of clear elastic and two 18"-long pieces of

flat lace. Gather one long edge of each lace piece until it measures 3" long. Draw inch marks on elastic. Pin each gathered lace edge to the middle inch of the marked elastic.

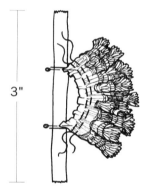

3"

5 Backstitch to secure lace to elastic; then sink needle. Pull each elastic "handle" to stretch elastic while you zigzag to lace. (No other type of elastic will stretch this far.)

6 Fold elastic handles to wrong side; then lap and securely hand-sew elastic ends together. Slide each elasticized lace ruffle over pillow's end ruffles.

7 Wrap square or rectangular doily around pillow and tack to fabric cover at doily's four corners.

*"**A**fter trying diligently to whiten this linen, I gave up and dyed it gray along with this spare pillowcase edging. They look spectacular against the black velvet pillow."*
—Gaye Kriegel

For the Table

You may own, inherit, or purchase old linens designed for table use and (surprise!) actually use them as they were intended—as tablecloths, placemats, and napkins. But if that doesn't suit your lifestyle, don't just store these linens away—use them around the house in ways that do not require any manipulation or sewing. (See *No-Sew Ideas*, page 4.) You could still retrieve them should you decide to host a formal dinner party later this decade—or next.

Lace and flowers are a tried-and-true pairing that can be relied upon to add simple elegance to any table. Vase Sleeves are an example of this classic combination, and do not require the linens to be cut.

Small pieces of linens, leftover from other *Affordable Heirlooms* projects, provide a perfect complement to any subject set inside the Patchwork Picture Frame.

Vase Sleeves

Further enhance a beautiful vase, disguise a damaged one, or recycle other containers with these simple vase sleeves, made from hankies. The vases are lovely, either left empty or filled with fresh, dried, or silk flowers (see Resources, page 115), or other decorations. Change hankies, ribbon colors, or vase contents for a centerpiece to suit any special occasion or holiday. Notice how each style of Vase Sleeve emphasizes a particular hankie embellishment, whether it's a single motif, embroidered border, or lace edging (similar to the Hankie Collars starting on page 27). Several vases can be grouped for impact or each can stand alone.

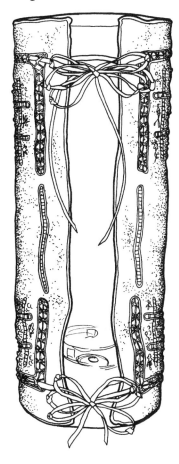

Border Vase Sleeve

Procedure

1 Weave narrow ribbon through open embroidered spaces along hankie's upper and lower edges.

2 Wrap hankie around cylinder-style container (edges will gap, meet, or overlap at front, depending on vase's circumference), and hold temporarily with a rubber band. Pull ribbon tightly; then knot and shape into bows.

3 If hankie slips down or gaps after rubber band is removed, secure in a few places with tiny pieces of double-sided tape.

Kerchief Vase Sleeve ✂

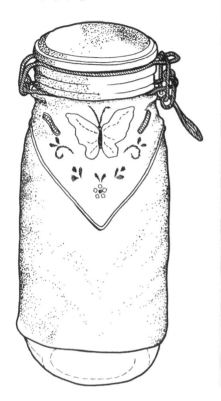

Procedure

1 Fold down embellished corner of hankie, and slip a ribbon under the fold. Opposite hankie corner may be folded under, if hankie is longer than container.

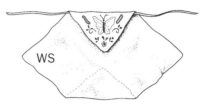

WS

2 Wrap hankie around cylinder-style container, and tie ribbon in back. Pin together, then hand-sew remaining hankie corners in back, to ensure a tight fit against container.

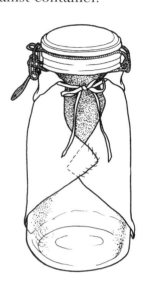

Lace-Edged Vase Sleeve ✂

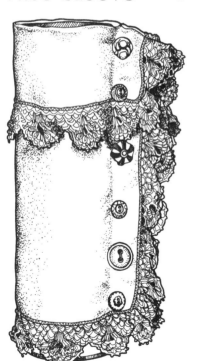

Procedure

1 Wrap hankie around cylinder-style container, folding down hankie's top edge, if necessary, to equal container height. Cinch excess hankie along container's side, and pin snugly.

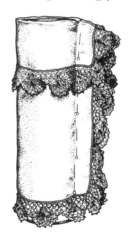

2 Hand-sew matching or assorted buttons through hankie layers, having button edges right next to container. Remove pins.

Patchwork Picture Frame

Surround your subject with small pieces of leftover linens by purchasing a precut frame kit or making your own frame. Consider designing specific linen and photo combinations, such as pink or blue linens for a baby's picture, red and green embroidery on white linens for the family Christmas portrait, or Great-Grandma's heirloom picture framed with her hankie. Techniques similar to the Patchwork Picture Frame, may be used to cover a box or photo album.

Supplies

- ruler, graph paper, pencil, scissors
- 2 pieces of cardboard the size of finished frame
- cardboard for easel (frame's standing support)
- batting the size of finished frame
- embellished linen pieces for front cover
- lightweight fabric for front cover underlining, frame back, and easel
- glue, such as Aleene's Thick Designer "Tacky" Glue
- clothespins
- ribbon scrap

Pattern

1 Determine frame opening size by measuring 1/8" smaller than picture all around. Draw opening in center of graph paper.

2 Draw a border from 1" to 3" wide around center opening for finished frame size. Trim paper to this line and cut out center opening.

3 Draw a rectangle for the easel pattern, 2" wide by two-thirds the frame height.

Procedure

1 Trace the frame pattern's perimeter twice onto cardboard; then cut. Trace and cut out center opening on *one* cardboard for frame; cut batting identical to frame, and glue together. Reserve other cardboard for backing.

2 Lay frame cardboard on double layer of fabric, and cut fabric 1" larger all around. Use one fabric piece as front cover underlining, and reserve the other to cover backing.

3 Pin linen pieces onto underlining, using finished linen edges to overlap and cover the cut linen edges. Edgestitch along linen edges through all thicknesses.

4 Center padded side of frame on wrong side of embellished underlining. To miter outside corners, cut excess fabric 1/4" beyond cardboard tips. Fold and glue the 1/4" allowance over cardboard tips.

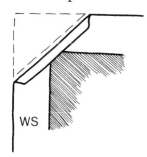

WS

5 Fold and glue fabric edges around cardboard's perimeter.

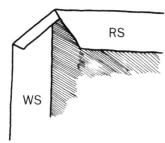

RS

WS

6 Trim excess fabric from frame center, leaving a 1/2" allowance on each side. Clip into corners, wrap, and then glue edges to cardboard.

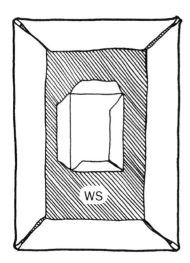

WS

7 Optional lace edging may be added now around frame opening or extending from behind frame perimeter.

8 Cover backing cardboard with fabric as described earlier (disregard opening). Glue frame and backing, wrong sides together, along bottom and sides. *Do not* glue top edge. Hold temporarily with clothespins until glue dries.

9 Trace and then cut easel pattern from cardboard. Score cardboard 1" from one short end. Lay cardboard along a folded piece of fabric, and cut fabric 1/4" wider on three sides.

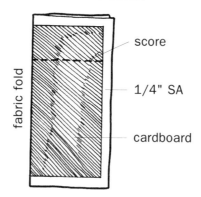

fabric fold

score

1/4" SA

cardboard

10 Fold under 1/4" along one short end. Fold fabric in half lengthwise, right sides together, and sew the long side and across bottom (leaving top folded edge open).

WS

11 Turn fabric right sides out, and insert cardboard. Hand-sew or glue fabric opening closed. Glue easel's scored end to frame back, midway between sides, and even with bottom. Glue ribbon scrap between frame back and easel to stabilize.

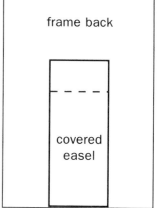

frame back

covered easel

12 Insert picture between top edges of frame and backing, into position behind frame opening.

"I thought these were Edna's relatives but it was just a picture that she liked and bought."
—Gaye Kriegel

Affordable Heirlooms

For the Wall

Framing is a way to pay homage to valued linens. If the linen has personal significance, write the details on paper, and glue it to the frame's backing paper, to benefit future generations.

Your combination of linen, fabric, and frame can make the project suitable for hanging in any room. You can frame a linen which has been mounted on fabric, or frame a collage of linen pieces underneath the shaped opening of a fabric-covered board.

Linens

To prepare the linen, refer to *Finding and Caring for Linens,* page 1.

Square the linen somewhat during pressing, but don't try too much if it's old. Consider making minor repairs, such as re-attaching a lace edging, using a fine needle and embroidery-weight thread to match the linen.

Carefully trim any stray threads from the back of transparent linens, to prevent threads from showing through when linen is mounted. Check to see if the embroidery has a one-way design. If only one corner is embellished, decide where to position that corner, perhaps hanging the frame diagonally.

Frames

If you have a rectangular or oval linen, try a ready-made frame that provides an equal margin all around. If your linen is square or circular, a rectangular ready-made frame may look awkward.

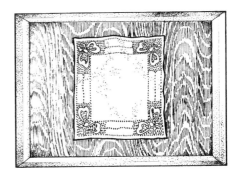

Consider overlapping the linen with mementos, such as pictures, postcards and lace pieces to fill the wider margins, as well as cover tears or stains. A custom-sized frame is a more expensive option.

Adding glass to the frame reduces the textural appeal of fabrics, but protects against dust, smoke, and fingers. Use spacers to prevent the glass from resting directly on the linen.

A shadow-box frame separates the glass from your linen, and allows the addition of three-dimensional objects, such as buttons or gloves.

Fabric

Like a stage backdrop, the fabric plays an important role in defining the character of the project, from casual to formal, simple to elegant, whimsical to dignified.

Velvet or moiré are beautiful fabric choices, but muslin or calico could be appropriate for some projects. Should you ever disassemble your framed linen, Kaethe Kliot of Lacis (see Resources, page 115) warns that dark velvet lint embedded in lace could cause permanent staining. Like your linen, fabric may have a one-way design to consider. The more color contrast between linen and fabric, the more dramatic the result.

Framed Hankie ✂

Please read the general information at the beginning of this section. With design decisions made, assembly may begin.

Procedure

1 Cut a cardboard or foam-core board to fit frame. Cut mounting fabric a few inches larger than cardboard, to allow for wrapping to the back. To pad surface, cut batting same size as cardboard.

2 Layer cardboard, optional batting, fabric, and frame together. Pin in place the linen(s) and anything else that will be sewn onto fabric. (Glued items can be added later.) Remove frame, and sew items to mounting fabric, using a fine needle and embroidery-weight thread to match linen. Small, lightweight linens may need only to be tacked in places, not sewn all around.

3 Reposition mounting fabric onto cardboard; then turn over onto a clean surface. Wrap fabric around outside edges to back, folding excess at corners, and secure with tape or glue. Add any glued-on items to front.

4 Insert cardboard into frame (glass optional), and secure with small finishing nails or tape. Glue a paper cover to frame back, if desired, and attach hardware for hanging.

*"**T**his is my wedding invitation and a hankie given to me by my mother-in-law."*
—Edna Powers

Linen Silhouette

Make your collage somewhat larger than your silhouette opening, and then edgestitch linens together. Tape perimeter of collage to a piece of poster board.

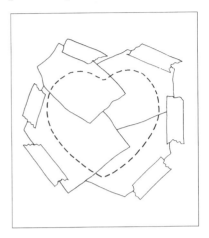

Please read the general information at the beginning of this section. In addition to those design considerations, decide on the shape of your silhouette opening. Choose a shape that is easy to recognize from its outline, such as a heart, oval, flower, rabbit, or cat. Remember, the more complicated the shape, the more difficult it will be to cut the opening and then to cover it with fabric.

Procedure

1 Cut mat board (preferably acid-free) to fit frame, and then cut silhouette opening in center. Batting may be added to pad either the mat board or the silhouette opening.

2 Cut fabric a few inches larger than mat board. Wrap fabric around outside edges to back, folding excess at corners, and secure with tape or glue. Cut excess fabric from silhouette opening, leaving at least a 1/2"-wide margin (wider, if your fabric ravels easily). Clip margin as necessary to wrap fabric to back side of opening, and secure with tape or glue.

3 Collect an assortment of linen pieces, especially those salvaged from otherwise unusable linens. Pin pieces together, using finished edges to overlap cut edges.

4 Center and tape poster board under silhouette opening. Place into frame (glass optional), add backing cardboard for support, and secure with small finishing nails or tape. Glue a paper cover to frame back, if desired, and attach hardware for hanging.

For the Window

Lace of any kind hanging in a window casts lovely twinkling shadows as light is filtered into a room. Lace-edged pillowcases, tablecloths, and European guest towels often provide enough yardage to cover a window. Smaller linens, such as hankies or napkins, can be put into service as a valance or as tieback.

Certain windows receive a tremendous amount of sun exposure, which can cause rapid deterioration of linens. Consider the added protection of a lining, pull-down shades, or blinds for at least part of the day.

Curtain styles vary from flat (without any fullness) to gathered (with any preferred amount of fullness), although the linens, varied as they are, typically dictate this decision despite your preference.

Be sure linens are preshrunk, to prevent curtain from being too short after the first cleaning.

A variety of rods is available, from simple spring rods that are concealed inside the curtain casing, to any creative support you can imagine.

Curtains

For each variation below, measure for curtain's finished length, add a casing allowance that will easily slip over selected rod, and then cut off any excess linen. Sew a casing along curtain's upper edge.

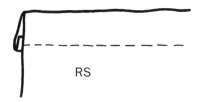

RS

To increase usable linen length, another fabric or bias tape may be added for the casing.

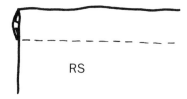

RS

Using Pillowcases

Procedure

1 Cut off the seam opposite pillowcase opening. Because some pillowcases are woven without seams, decide whether to cut pillowcase open along side or center back—whichever way uses embellishment best.

2 Hem each side edge, and sew a casing along what is now the upper curtain edge. Matching pillowcases can hang on each side of a window.

3 For a wider single curtain, sew two matching pillowcases together, and hide the seam with an edge-stitched ribbon. Add identical ribbons at curtain sides, for visual balance.

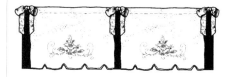

Using Tablecloths

Procedure

1 Use three finished sides of a tablecloth as the curtain's sides and hem. Cut off excess along fourth edge. Sew casing along upper curtain edge.

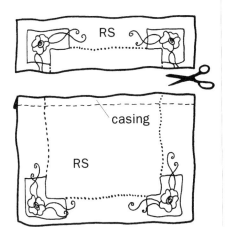

2 The cut-off portion may be enough to make a matching valance, by turning that piece upside down, and sewing another casing along its cut edge.

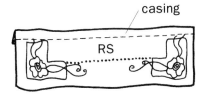

Using European Guest Towels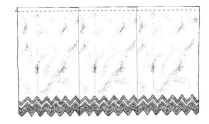

Increase usable width for a curtain by seaming together three European guest towels. These seams will be partially disguised in curtain gathers and will not look inappropriate, as one center seam would. Sew a casing along the upper edge.

Valances

Valances may be shorter versions of curtain techniques described above. Also like curtains, valances can be flat or have fullness. Try using one of these ideas as the top ruffle of a fabric shower curtain.

Hankies or napkins, matching or assorted, can become an interesting valance. Sew them together side-by-side, either with traditional seams or with an overlap-and-topstitch technique. If linens are not identically sized, match the lower edges; then cut them even at the top before sewing casing.

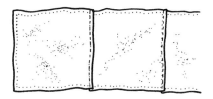

Hankies or napkins may also be sewn together diagonally, tip-to-tip. Overlap as much as you prefer to create the look you want, and to fit the window. Tack bottom points of each hankie together, and then slip valance over curtain rod.

Try draping one or more hankies or napkins over the top edge of a curtain, as an accent.

Tiebacks

✂ For no-sew and no-cut curtain tiebacks, fold a hankie in half diagonally, tie kerchief-style around curtain, and then secure tied knot at wall.

To recycle the lace edging from a pillowcase, cut enough lace to wrap around curtain, lap and glue cut ends together, slip around curtain, and then secure joined lace ends to wall.

To make a pair of tiebacks from a tea towel, cut it in half lengthwise. Then sew each half into a turned tube loop, following construction directions for the Toilet Paper Sling on page 86. Adjust size of loop, topstitch through all thicknesses, slip tieback over curtain, and then secure at wall.

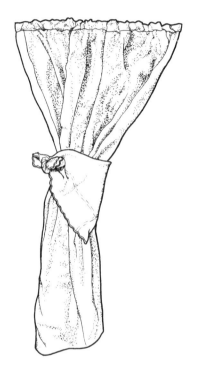
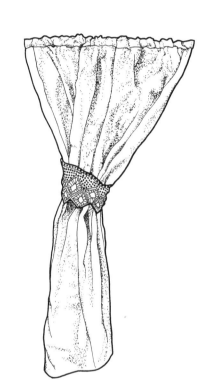
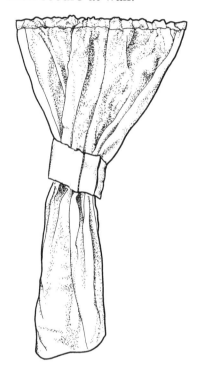

"My childhood bedroom was so overabundantly lavished in lace that I hated it. Gradually, as an adult, the more I learned about lace, the more it fascinated me. Now I'm surrounded by lace once more—5,000 square feet of it, floor to ceiling."
—Kaethe Kliot, owner of Lacis in Berkeley, California

Conclusion

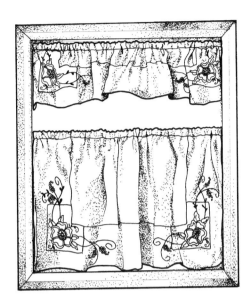

So dear reader, consider this book your window into the world of *Affordable Heirlooms.* We have tried to welcome you, inspire you, and teach you how these extraordinary textiles deserve a second chance to be as useful as they are enriching to our lives. Whether your search for linens leads you to your own closet or around the world, we believe that you will enjoy their beauty, marvel at their workmanship, appreciate their uniqueness, and be delighted with the opportunity for creativity that each linen has to offer. Feel free to share your experiences with us through letters and photographs. We look forward to hearing from you.

Edna Powers and Gaye Kriegel
c/o Open Chain Publishing
PO Box 2634-AH
Menlo Park, CA 94026

Acknowledgments

We extend our thanks to:

Robbie Fanning and Chilton for the opportunity to write this book

William and Susan Grindley for allowing us to photograph in their beautiful Victorian home

FREEZEFRAME (See Resources, page 115.) for providing freeze-dried flowers and vegetables for photographs

Yarn Tree Designs (See Resources, page 115.) for donating triple-fold greeting cards

Joann Collins and Ginny Strametz for donating linens

Loura Dashiell for hair and makeup service for photographs

for modeling:

Rosa Almazan
Sharon Andersen
Barbara Bowers
Johanna DiCecco
April Gooding
Alison Gordy
Lindsey Gordy
Cassie Kalenda
Chelsea Kalenda
Genna Kriegel
Patti Lyter
Kendra Nichols
Kerry Nichols
Andrea Perea
Kimberlee Powers

for contributing anecdotes:

Carol Ahles
Barbara Bowers
Lenora Brancato
Elizabeth Bringmann
Gail Brown
Clotilde
Joann Collins
Jackie Dodson
Janice Ferguson
Edith Forsling
Marilyn Green
Doris Hoover
Debra Justice
Kaethe Kliot
Carla Lopez
Mary Mulari
Kimberlee Powers
Jan Saunders
B. J. Tichinin
Nancy Zieman

Bibliography

Collecting Antique Linens, Lace, and Needlework, Johnson, Frances. Wallace-Homestead, 1991, ISBN 0-87069-633-5 —easy reading, historical background and collecting guide.

Innovative Sewing, Brown, Gail and Tammy Young. Chilton Book Company, 1990, ISBN 0-8019-7999-4—quick, interesting ideas on many sewing topics.

The Linen Closet: How to Care for Your Fine Linens and Lace, Clise, Michele Durkson. Marquand Books, Inc., 1992, ISBN 0-8118-0196-9—concise, usable information on caring for linens.

Linens and Lace, Foley, Tricia. Clarkson N. Potter, 1990, ISBN 0-517-57680-5 —resources and inspiring photographs.

Old Glories, Magical Makeovers for Vintage Textiles, Trims and Photos, Herbort, Diane, and Susan Greenhut. EPM Publications, 1992, ISBN 0-939009-62-5—entertaining blend of history, humor, and how-to

Victorian Fancywork, Markrich, Lilo, and Heinz Edgar Kiewe. Henry Regnery Co., 1974, ISBN 0-8092-8348-4—fascinating description of Victorian life.

Resources

acid-free tissue paper and boxes, linens, books
Lacis
2982-AH Adeline Street
Berkeley, CA 94703
510-843-7178

freeze-dried flowers and vegetables
FREEZEFRAME
6216-AH Hoke Road
Clayton, OH 45315
513-854-8506

mail-order linens
Grannies Heartstrings
PO Box 1756-AH
Morgan Hill, CA 95038-1756
408-779-3287

mail-order linens
Hill Country Interests
3426-AH San Saba Drive
San Jose, CA 95148-2158

pattern paper
The Sewing Place
PO Box 111446-AH
Campbell, CA 95011
408-252-8444
800-LV-SEWERS

sewing supplies
Nancy's Notions
P.O. Box 683
Beaver Dam, WI 53916
800-833-0690

Clotilde
2 Sew Smart Way
Stevens Point, WI 54481-8031
800-772-2891

triple-fold greeting cards
Yarn Tree Designs
117-AH Alexander Avenue
Ames, IA 50010
800-247-3952

Index